The Hamster Won't Die

A Treasury of Feral Humor

Whitney Collins

ISBN 978-1-300-20904-1

For Robbie, with love and gratitude

(And also Mark Zuckerberg. But mostly Mickey Rourke.)

FOREWORD/FAQs

What is this book?

It's a collection of some of my published humor pieces, which
have appeared on *The Huffington Post* (only one piece appeared
over there, but you better believe I will milk that for all it's
worth), *HowAboutWe*, *McSweeney's Internet Tendency*, *The Big Jewel*,
Loop, *errant parent*, *The Yellow Ham*, and my blog *The Unpoet* (which
I never update and no one reads). In short, a compendium of
things better left unsaid.

Why did you self publish?

For the same reason people cut their own hair: I am impatient,
shameless, and I have a party to go to. (Actually, there's no party,
but I am turning 40, and you can drop off some Trader Joe's
hummus if you feel so inclined.)

Why the title?

I was originally going to call the book *Poster Child*, because of all
the posting I do on the Internet, but then I discovered that name
had already been taken by a book that's literally about the
saddest thing in the world -- a child amputee. I didn't want to
take the chance that *this* book (the second saddest thing in the
world) might get confused with *that* book, so, my next obvious
choices for titles were: *Read This, Become A Billionaire* and *Everything
You NEVER Wanted to Know About Johnny Depp* and, lastly, *Lots and*

Lots of High-Resolution Pictures of Prince Harry's A$$. I finally chose *The Hamster Won't Die*, because our hamster won't die.

What does "feral humor" mean?
Domestic-ish comedy that has been banished to the backyard with nothing more than a rusty water bowl and an expired rabies shot. Or a literary version of our cat, Casper. Don't pet him.

How often do you write?
About every 27 minutes.

Why is humor important?
Humor has three jobs. One, to fill us with the sort of joy that brings us closer to the innate divinity of the Universe. Two, to reveal humanity's foolishness through cold, painful truths that instill us with humility. Three, poop jokes.

What do you do in your spare time?
I make bookmarks out of bacon strips.

Why does this book not have a Table of Contents?
Because the book is made up of like 100 or so humor pieces, not, say, 15 chapters, and the Table of Contents started to look like one of those overwhelming and irritating 40-page menus you get at a sushi restaurant. I knew I was going to lose readers in the

hand roll section before they even got to the noodle part. And the noodle part is somewhat redeeming.

Did you know there are typos and grammatical errors in this book?
That was intentional. You know how someone will buy a brand-new dresser and then beat the shit out of it with a hammer to make it look old? Well, that's how I handle self-publishing. It's sort of a "shabby chic" technique. (Honestly, I don't know if there are mistakes in this book, but I'm pretty sure there will be, and it will really bum me out, because I'm pretty anal, so I'm just going to go on and make some mistakes hear two insure its knot prefect.) Also: there are no odd page numbers. On purpose. Maybe.

Why all the gratuitous sarcasm and profanity?
This book serves as a vehicle for me to get my ya-yas out. No worries, my next book is about Victorian cross-stitching.

What if I want a refund?
If you don't like the paper version of this book, you can burn it and it will smell like s'mores.* If you don't like the electronic version of this book, you can shake your e-reader and it will turn into an Etch A Sketch.*

*lies

I have no discernible hairstyle.

-- David Spade

WOULD YOU LIKE YOUR RECEIPT IN THE BAG?

Would I like my receipt in the bag? Is that what you asked? WOULD I LIKE MY RECEIPT IN THE BAG? Wow. What a charitable and utterly observant question you've asked. You obviously have the ocular finesse of a peregrine falcon and the mental capacity of a dolphin. (I'm sorry. Did I say dolphin? I meant manatee. A manatee with a propeller sticking out of its forehead.)

But back to the question: Would I like my receipt in the bag? Well, seeing that the left side of my body, from armpit to thumb, is balancing a 30-pound baby, a diaper bag, a bottle of Purell, 11 pretzel rods, and a blanket that the general public frequently mistakes for a tuna net. And seeing that the right side of my body is commandeering a wallet, a phone, a keychain, six (somebody help this woman) panty liners, and a pair of (where the buttmunch did THESE come from?) pruning shears, I don't think the bag is the right place for the receipt at all.

No, sir.

Instead, if it's not too much trouble, I'd like for you to roll the receipt (tightly, please) into a small scroll and then place that scroll into my right ear. Sort of like a Q-tip. I think it's quite practical if you ask me, but I'm sure we can think of other completely logical places the receipt might like to go. Other than inside my EAR CANAL.

Hmmm. I have an idea. How about we fold the receipt into a tiny airplane? Then, while I'm staggering toward the door with all this shit I came in with, plus all the shit I just bought, you can fly that little airplane to me. But be sure to aim it a little ahead of me. That way it'll be easier for me to catch between my front teeth.

Or how about this? This'll be really fun! Why don't I grab one of these pull-back-and-release, $7.50 toy cars that you savants sell by the register? The impulse ones that are covered in Chinese lead and cause Parkinson's? Why don't we put the receipt in the way-back of one of these little Lexus SUVs and then put it on the floor and then I can pull it back and release it -- OH, SAY, 85 TIMES -- out the door and down the sidewalk and through the parking lot and then to my car. I'm pretty sure I can handle that. Can you also add a couple of lawn chairs to my tab and strap them to my back? No, no need to get the door for me. My hands may be full, but I can always carry something on my tailbone. In fact, grab me that baby pool. No. The big one.

Or maybe this: how 'bout we take that receipt and burn it! And then we take the ashes of the receipt and put them in a little urn! Do you sell tiny urns here? No? No urns?! WHAT KIND OF A

14

SHITFORBRAINS DRUGSTORE DOES NOT SELL MINIATURE CREMATORY VESSELS? Well, then, I guess I'm going to have to buy this tin of Altoids and then pour them all into my mouth until my pancreas screams its way out of my rectum. Then, when I've finally regained consciousness, we can put the ashes of the receipt into this now-empty, handy-dandy Altoids tin and you and I can get a couple of tickets to Hawaii where we'll go to sprinkle the ashes. I'm pretty sure that's what the receipt would want. To be sprinkled in the Hanauma Bay. Do you have time next week to fly to Hawaii? No?

YOU DICK.

Okay, then. Plan E. Let's crinkle the receipt into a ball and then you give me a straw and I'll blow through the straw and keep the wadded-up receipt-ball afloat until I get to my accountant's office. Do you also have a potato sack and a spoon with an egg and a Slip'N Slide? Because we could just go on and turn this whole thing into a field day.

Or, on second thought, why not call a taxi to come pick up the receipt and then send the taxi to my house? Here's my address. Just tell the cab driver to wait for me. I'm sure it will be expensive cab fare, but I'll do anything for that receipt. He's done so much for me. That receipt is like family. That is, if family is a crappy piece of paper that you'd be happy seeing a hobo use for a testicle-bandage.

Or here's one: put the receipt in an envelope and mail it to your boss as proof you should die a very slow and very painful death while I look on eating popcorn and CRYING.

(Crying because I'm laughing so hard.)

Or maybe we should just cover the receipt in peanut butter and bird seed and let a small woodland animal eat it. We could feed it to the next black-footed ferret that comes into this Rite Aid, and then we can put the ferret into a cage and take him to my home office where we can wait for him to shit the receipt out into my 2012 tax file. Because, in addition to the bag being a super-stupid place to put the receipt, I also really need to KEEP the receipt. I'll certainly need it for tax time later this year. Because I'll need to write these diapers and cheap wine off as work expenses. That's what I do, you see. I change diapers and drink. These are OFFICE SUPPLIES I've bought today at your fine neighborhood drugstore that employs assbags like yourself who are too smart for Mensa. IMPORTANT OFFICE SUPPLIES.

Anyway. I can see the line is getting long. There are lots of sad-looking people here waiting to buy *OK! Magazine* and vodka and Kit Kats.

So, to finally answer your question: YES.

YES, I'D LIKE MY RECEIPT IN THE BAG.

Because I'm assuming by "in the bag" you mean "up your ass."

WELL, THIS IS AWKWARD

The Vietnamese lady

Who does spray tans

Always says

Take off bra!

And I'm like no thanks

And she's like

What you say? Take off bra!

And I'm like no thanks

And she's like

YOU BE SORRY!

YOU

WILL

HAVE

LINES!

Take. Off. Bra.

And I'm like

Apparently NO THANKS means PLEASE ASK ME AGAIN

AND AGAIN AND AGAIN UNTIL MY EARS ARE

PROFUSELY BLEEDING

And then

A hush falls over the spray tan room

Just the two of us in that

Cold

Brown

Closet that smells of coconut

Or is it curry?

Tell me again…

(Actually, I think it's cumin.)

…who do I have to pay around here for some orange thighs?

TRUCK NUTS

Whenever I see these on a vehicle

I think

When can I meet the owner of this truck?

Will he have enough time

In his intellectually demanding life

To spare me a few pearls of wisdom?

When can I ask him questions that plague humanity?

Such as

What is the meaning of life?

What is your truck's name?

Where do you get your chest waxed?

Also:

Do they make a female version of these?

God knows

I'd like some ovaries for my van

(But not life-sized

Because then I'd just have another set of earrings)

NEW OLD WIVES' TALES

If someone dies on Good Friday, they go directly to heaven. If someone dies on Fat Tuesday, they probably had diabetes.

If your nose itches, a fool is about to kiss you. If your crotch itches, blame Derek.

Be sure to wait an hour after eating before dumpster diving.

If you carry an acorn in your pocket, good luck will follow you wherever you go. If you carry a lamb chop, the same holds true. Except you can replace good luck with possum.

Never, ever lay a hat on a bed. Unless it's a blond, inflatable sombrero.

Make a wish on the first robin of spring. If you finish wishing before the robin flies away, you're not greedy enough. Who convinced you to reach so low? Man, you're a real, underachieving asshole. I don't know how you look at yourself in the mirror. Hey, look! A robin!

Grapefruit at dawn, live real long. Steak for dinner, bad gas.

Always bury your fingernail clippings under a full moon; if it doesn't get rid of your plantar warts, it'll get rid of that perfectly nice guy you've been dating. You know, Derek.

Feed a cold, starve your son's guinea pig.

If you dream of fish, you're pregnant. If you dream of fish sticks, your mother wishes you'd never been born.

Never walk under a ladder. Unless, of course, it's wearing a diaper.

An apple a day keeps the blood-sucking, well-endowed, super-sexy vampire-robots away.

If you say goodbye to a friend on a bridge, you will never see each other again. Probably because it's that "friend" whose boyfriend you borrowed and she's been hoping to get you on a bridge for a couple of years now. See ya.

Housecats can't suck the breath from a newborn, but they will steal your condoms.

The child that is born on the Sabbath day is fair and wise and good and gay. (Not Rosie O'Donnell gay. More like Portia de Rossi gay.)

If the eyes are the windows to the soul, then the navel is the peephole to the lint.

The knuckle-bone from a piece of mutton was once thought to be a preventative charm against rheumatism. A bison's bladder, filled with M&M'S and worn about the neck, will probably get you that nanny job.

Chewing gum takes seven years to get out of your pubic hair.

In German lore, if you sneeze three times before breakfast, you'll receive a present by day's end. If you sneeze four times, Hitler's ghost will piss in your oatmeal.

Red sky at night? Sailor's delight. Red sky at morning? What a delicious peyote Danish this is!

If the first baby calf of spring is born all white, you'd better have your lawyer draw up a living will. Be sure to have a lengthy discussion about feeding tubes.

A rabbit's foot, dyed the colors of your favorite NFL team and made into a keychain, pretty much makes you a cruel bastard. So does a jockstrap made of veal.

If you put a cabbage leaf in your underwear, well, then, so will I.

Lucky omens: a magpie, a shoelace knot, a penny, a chimney sweep. Unlucky omens: a black cat, a shotgun between the shoulder blades, a layover at the Pittsburgh airport, heart disease.

A cricket in the house is really fucking disgusting.

Every time Derek rings a bell, a Kevin Bacon movie comes on TBS.

(Originally appeared in a similar form on The Big Jewel*)*

AN OUTDOOR CAT IS A JOY FOREVER

The last time I cleaned a litter box

I didn't find any rubies

So, hey

Pussy cat

(Or should I take the cat off of that)

Until you shit me a solitaire

Enjoy the garage

PUT THAT IN YOUR TOY BANJO AND SMOKE IT

Oh

Taylor

Taylor

Taylor Swift

You think it's so cute

To make a heart

With your hands

But

You know what's cuter?

Keith Richards

Making a liver

Out of a tube sock.

ODE TO AN EPISIOTOMY

Oh, give me a frontal lobotomy,

Not another episiotomy.

Cause funny it ain't,

For me or my taint.

This procedure, illegal, it outta be.

Dear Doctor, I beg: pretty please

For a c-section's relative ease,

Instead of a cut --

From my hoo-hah to butt -- What?!?!?

You give me a stress ball to squeeze?!?!

When your child has a 15-inch skull,

Request vodka and Xanax to dull,

Then prepare for a push

That renders your tush

Completely and utterly null.

To illustrate this for a man,

Shove some dynamite up in his can;

Crack a beer while you watch

The demise of his crotch,

Then ask him if he's going to breastfeed.

(That's right motherfuckers, I don't have to rhyme if I don't want to.)

Listen up, assholes and bitches,
After 65 tight-as-hell stitches,
I deserve diamonds!!
A transplanted hymen!!
And some Lanacane dammit! This itches!

So, before getting reamed by a rhino,
Get narcotics galore from your gyno.
Make out your will,
Take a handful of pills,
Smoke a bong, do some shots, be a wino.

But of course, in the end, it's all worth
The pain for the mirth of the birth.
But no one will blame you
Or call you insane if you
Decide to get your tubes tied, become a lesbian, and leave your family.

DEEEEEEEELISH

I'm finally going to share
Honeybaked Ham's secret ham salad recipe
That I had to make
When I was ham salad wench there in like 1990
Or was it 1991?

Ready?

One-third ham scraps
One-third sweet relish
One-third Miracle Whip

Put it all in a clean plastic trashcan
Put on one of those long rubber gloves they use to give a
pregnant mare a pelvic exam
(You know one of those gloves that goes up to your armpit?)

Now stir
Until you think you're going to die
Serve immediately

(Or not)

PHEW

I thought I was coming off
Crystal meth
Then I remembered I hadn't had
My fourth cup of coffee.

SPAM SEVEN WAYS

Seven common spam emails and suggested ways to respond.

Subject: <u>PLEASE ENDEAVOUR TO USE IT FOR GOD.</u>

Hello My Dearest, I know how surprise this email might appear but i want you to consider it as a request from a dying woman. My Name is Mrs. Elizabeth Wilson. from Israel but now undergoing medical treatment in Abidjan the capital city of Ivory Coast.

Recently, My Doctor told me that I may die due to cancer problem, though what disturbs me most is my stroke and deaf problem.

Haven known my condition i decided to Serve God with my wealth. Seven million six hundred thousand united states dollars. I want an individual that will use this fund to provide succour to the poor and indigent orphanages, widows. As soon as I receive your response I shall give you the contact of the Bank where the said fund is deposited.

-- Mrs.Elizabeth Wilson.

Suggested response: Wow, Liz! You've been through the wringer! Tell me more about your "stroke and deaf problem." I'm always interested in how horrible people suffer. Also. What kind of cancer do you have? Asshole cancer? Because you're an asshole.

Subject: Details Regarding Staying Healthy

A courtesy one-time public service message about Attention Deficit Hyperactivity Disorder (ADHD) and no further emails will be sent.

ADHD sometimes called ADD, is linked with hyperactivity, impulsiveness, and attention problems in both children and adults. It's estimated that up to 12% of children and 6% of adults have ADHD, making it harder for them to focus, manage their time, control their behavior, or even sit still.

Treatment is often a combination of medication and behavioral therapy. Take care.

Suggested response: Why would you think I'd be interested in an email about ADD or ADHD or hey does anyone have a recipe for pigeon stew here's a nickel maybe Tallahassee?

Subject: Hello

Hello, I am lovely Juliana,i drop at your profile,And I love what i saw there, i believe we can get acquainted if it interest you get back to me and more,i am cute,Accommodate,caring, and very lively,I need a man who posses all this Attributes.I have all the

Qualities that a man desires and Craves in a woman. You can contact me direct to my email address here for me to send you my pictures ok

Suggested response: Hi Juliana. I'm glad you drop at my profile. Mind if I ask which one? Because you obviously think I am a man, and I'm curious which shit picture of mine I need to soak with acid, set on fire, and drop into a septic tank. If it's my Facebook profile, I'll just have to go on and drink a handle of vodka and pass out on some railroad tracks, because that's my best photo ever.

Subject: Key Info In Regards to Staying Fit
A quick one-time public service announcement about Influenza (no further emails will be sent).

In any given year, it's estimated that 5 to 20% of Americans get influenza. In the United States, the flu kills about 36,000 people annually.

Flu symptoms include: High fever, vomiting, diarrhea, chills, fatigue, body aches, dry cough and runny nose. Be well.

Suggested response: Um. I think you sent me one of these before about ADD/ADHD. So, you lie. Also, what you describe is not the flu. It's testicular torsion.

Subject: RE:Receipt

___-----_----------_____----------------_____

==================

==================

DEAR SIR/MADAM

I wish to relate an important message concerning a huge business plan. Right now, I have a plan that could net over some huge amounts which i wish you to be part of it. If you are interested you can send me your details...Regards, Derr

Suggested response: Awesome! Thanks, Derr! Here are my details: 5'4" (in clogs), lactose intolerant, Capricorn rising.

I know you won't do me wrong, Derr, because any guy with a name that's synonymous with "duh," "no shit, Sherlock," and "doi," is obviously a financial wizard.

(Note the definition of "Derr" in the Urban Dictionary: [spinning a cat around in one hand] "DERR! Hi! I'm Rob. I'm the biggest idiot in the whole wide world!")

Also. Thanks for including all the dots and dashes at the top of your email. I thought my grandmother was sending me one of those "Prayer to St. Therese" emails that's been orbiting the earth since the commercialization of the Internet in 1995.

Subject: Important
I want you to claim some funds for me.Reply for details

Suggested response: Thanks for the brevity. And what a coincidence! I want you to claim something for me, too! If you pick up that Vera Bradley rolling duffel with the severed head in it at JFK, we'll call it even.

Subject: Hello Dearst One
My name is Mabel a pretty girl Living I Feel Empty without Can I Trust You, Am   approaching for you genuine friendshipand partnership Distance does not matter I believe true love further communication, please tell me more about yourself You sound very interesting I love to find out more about You I know that mycoming to You will result in happiness.

Suggested response: I find weasels both delicious and sexually attractive. Do you like the daytime soap *Satan Barbara*? How do you feel about someone who has very little money and also what the doctors say is an extra vertebra but really looks like a tail?

<u>Subject: Information Concerning Staying Fit</u>

A one-time awareness public service communication about Psoriasis (no further emails will be sent).

Psoriasis is a chronic, noncontagious immune condition that affects 5% of the US population. The most common form of Psoriasis is plaque psoriasis. Typical symptoms are red, itchy patches or spots, raised bumps, or silvery scales and can often be misdiagnoses as eczema. Take care.

Suggested response: Hi there, Derr. I'd like you to meet someone. Her name is Juliana and her mother, Mrs. Elizabeth Wilson, is LOADED. Just send me your details. Oh. And good luck with your testicles.

TIME FOR A RESTRAINING ORDER

Guess who showed up on my doorstep

Hoping I'd take him in

For like the tenth time this year?

The damn phone book.

How is he not dead yet?

GOOD THING I DIDN'T GET
THAT MASTER'S DEGREE

Have you ever played a game of Dot Arrow
With paper airplanes?

I didn't think so
Here are the rules:

First, hide with your plane
No
Not the blue one
this yellow one
NOOOOOO!!!!!!!!!
The other yellow one!!!!!
Aren't you listening?!?!?!?!?!

Now hide
But don't hide somewhere where I can kind of see you
Like in a door crack
Because that's creepy
Unless it's that big door crack in the bathroom door
That is the only one allowed

Also
I'm the only one who can jump out and scare people

People can't do that to me

Promise?

PROMISE?!?!?!?!?!?!?!

Then

Count to 20

But not fast 20

Sloooowwwww 20

Then

When I walk past where I think you're hiding

I throw this paper airplane

Right at your eye

Now

Don't forget the rules!!!

I SAID

DON'T FORGET THE RULES!!!!!!

Why aren't you standing on one leg?

That was a RULE!!!!!

(For what it's worth

I'm pretty sure Dot Arrow

Played more than once

Leads to alcoholism)

MY EIGHTH STROLLER

With my first child, I went through about seven strollers -- all of which could suck a whole cantaloupe through a coffee straw. Some of these pieces of shit were pawned off on me by older moms, a few were gifts from people I'm now pretty certain hated me, and one I bought from consignment; that particular stroller actually turned out to be fairly functional, despite the fact that it gave us all hand, foot and mouth disease and what we're just going to agree to call scabies.

So, when I found out I was expecting my second child, I decided this time around I'd find the perfect stroller, even if it cost more than Las Vegas fellatio and required me to drain myself of plasma.

For the final four months of my gestational period, I spent about 700 hours surfing the Web, reading customer opinions, and deciding which baby-mover to buy. It had to have a snack tray, a parent console, a 180-degree sunshade, full-recline capabilities, a lightweight frame, inflatable tires, rear-wheel suspension, an adjustable handle, a travel system, a peekaboo flap, a front swivel wheel, quick-folding abilities, a foot brake, water repellency, a safety leash, and a gear tray. I also wanted it in metallic coral, but I wasn't about to get picky. That's just not like me.

Anyway, I finally found it. This beaut had five-star reviews and all the crap I mentioned above. Plus, it even came with something called a "crotch restraint." Fabulous! I haven't known many whore-babies, but you can never be too safe.

Five weeks and $400 later, THE CHOSEN ONE arrived in all its polyester-and-fresh-rubber glory, and, after some minor assembly, I put the baby in that baby and set off to test drive my new Rolls.

Which turned out to feel more like a Kia.

I'm not gonna lie. I denied the stroller's suckage for a long time. I mean, if I ever meet George Clooney, and my husband allows me to sleep with George Clooney, I'm gonna sleep with George Clooney over and over and over again, even if it's horrible sex, because I'm just not going to be willing to admit that sex with George Clooney is horrible until the parent console breaks off of George Clooney. Because that's the final goddam straw, George! You can't look the way you look, and cost what you cost, and be THAT hard to fold up and put in the trunk!

UNACCEPTABLE.

So, I digress, but what I'm getting at is: FUCK YOU, STROLLER. It's been 10 months of trying to love you, and I'm finally ready to admit that I made a terrible mistake. You're impossible to push around, you move like you're drunk, and you always spill my drink. And that's not cheap vodka, dickweed! Also, I'm pretty sure your mother was a bitch-ass wheelbarrow who screwed an old ghetto shopping cart and pushed you outta her sweatshop vagina. Not to mention, your color was advertised as "Chili." Which looked like a lovely persimmon-maybe-shrimp bisque online. And seemed VERY CLOSE to coral, if not metallic coral. Well, you know what? You're not even close to CHILI. You're more like SCAB or TONSILLITIS or HEATHER PLACENTA. And I HATE you.

I know. I should probably write Customer Service a mature letter, explaining what is wrong with you and why I'm disappointed. (Because, hey! Free tire pump!) Or, I could take lots of pictures of your sagging, sun-damaged gear tray at the beach and send them to *US Weekly*. (I think that's what Clooney's ex-girlfriend did.) But instead, I've decided to douse you in jet fuel, set you on fire, video that shit, and post it on YouTube.

But not before I take the baby for a walk in you. It's a nice day out, and I was hoping you could sever one final finger of mine.

THE BABY HAS GAS

As the day draws to a close

And the sky turns the color of sherbet

And the baby and I sit on the porch swing

I am overcome with serenity

Until what can only be described as

The smell of 5,000 burning tractor tires

Catapults me face down onto the welcome mat

THE DREAM IS OVER

If my iPhone autocorrects "so" into "do"

One.

More.

Time.

I'm going to have to let the air out of

My Steve Jobs inflatable doll.

CONVERSATIONS WITH SIRI

Me: What is the weather going to be like today?

Siri: Today is Tuesday.

Me: I would like a cappuccino.

Siri: Finding directions to Mendocino.

Me: Farmer's Market.

Siri: I don't know what you mean by "farm and hairnet."

Me: FARRR-MERRRR'S MARRR-KETT!!!!

Siri: All right. Marquette University.

Me: Call Robbie.

Siri: Calling Bobby McFlanahan.

Me: NOOOOOOOOOOOOOO!!!! Not Bobby!

Siri: I'm sorry. I don't know what you mean by "knob hobby."

Me: Baby formula.

Siri: Here are two Formula 1 websites.

Me: Are you on drugs?

Siri: Filling your prescription at Walgreens.

Me: What's on the calendar?

Siri: Here's a recipe for chicken coriander.

Me: JESUS!

Siri: The Mormon church is one block away.

Me: How do you like it, Siri? Huh? In the armpit? In the armpit, you whore?

Siri: I found seven equestrian stables nearby.

Me: I said WHORE, dammit!! Not HORSE. WHORE!

Siri: Calling Ann Taylor Loft.

Me: WHAT??!?!?!?

Siri: Calling Ann Taylor Loft.

Me: GAHHHHHHHH!!

Siri: OK. Now I understand. Calling the Gap.

Me: Oh my God!! Help me, Siri! I think I'm having a stroke! Call an ambulance! Call 9-1-1!

Siri: Tomorrow will be partly to mostly cloudy.

Me: Die, Siri, die!! I hope you die a lonely robot death in the middle of cyberspace and that your tin soul screams in agony for all of eternity!!! I hope you choke on your own motherboard!!!

Siri: I'm sorry. I think you said "cheese Danish?"

FEW PEOPLE CAN ROCK
THE TRANSITIONS LENSES

When Mickey Rourke
Updates his status to:
Insomnia sucks
At the exact same time I have insomnia
I can't help but think we have more in common
Than just being decent wrestlers

Sometimes I wonder
What his favorite cereal is
And if it would be weird to send him
200 boxes of it

(I'm pretty sure it's Marlboro Pops)

Hey
Mickey

My friend said she saw you
In the Chelsea Bed Bath & Beyond
Looking at feather pillows
While you held a teacup chihuahua
And wore shiny gold Pumas
And socks that said

Suck My Dick

Just let me know
If you're looking for someone
To needlepoint that on a belt for you

I have a friend who might be interested

I DON'T KNOW HOW I KNOW THIS

How many blonds

Does it take

To see

If the stovetop is still hot?

One.

One to touch it.

FIVE THINGS YOU SHOULD NEVER
HAVE AT YOUR WEDDING

A Long Ceremony

I went to a wedding once (we'll call it the nuptials of Dick and Regina) that lasted longer than the coronation of Queen Elizabeth II. It involved a wedding party of 34, 775 guests, 18 prayers, eight performances on flute, lute, harp, cello, dulcimer, steel banjo, children's xylophone, and maybe even armpit farting, two priests, a Protestant minister, ten readings (some Cherokee, some Shel Silverstein), a gong, a rabbi, a boys' choir, a hologram of Tupac, confetti, widespread fainting, and Deep Vein Thrombosis.

I remember leaving the wedding to head to the reception, thinking: Gin. I need someone to get me gin. What's the fastest way to get gin in my bloodstream? Through my eye? Someone pour gin in my eyes!

I also remember thinking: I hate Dick and Regina.

The only thing that got me through that ceremony was imagining Forrest Gump shouting "Run! Run, Dick, run!" And then imagining Dick running far, far away from Regina, until the braces came off his legs.

So, you know. Keep it reasonable people. Fourteen minutes is more than adequate.

Babies and Animals

Babies and animals are adorable, but they cannot control their voices or bladders. Let's keep them where they belong: on Hallmark calendars. That is, unless you want your wedding to be remembered for the boy who dropped trou halfway down the aisle and urinated in the rose petal basket. Or for the doves that were released only to release an entire flockload of birdshit on people in strapless dresses. Or for the doggy in the doggy tux that ran out of the church, was blinded by his doggy top hat, and was run over by a limousine.

The one exception for this rule is capuchin monkeys. Boy, are they ever cute! If you can train several dozen of them to dress as little genies and deliver margaritas without throwing turds or transmitting Ebola, go for it!

Veal and Vegannaise

A wedding ceremony is not the time to announce how incredibly cruel or how amazingly thoughtful you are through food. No one wants harp seal kabobs any more than they want a tease-burger. So, stick with the chicken breasts and green beans and mashed potatoes. Or, if you're inviting me, steak and lobster.

Favors

What is UP with the FAVORS? You're giving everyone a big-ass free party, and they're giving you a toaster, so let's call the damn thing even. Do you know how time-consuming assembling favors is? I have seen mothers and daughters try to glue gun one another's mouths closed over favors. In fact, there should be a reality show called HUGE FAVORS, in which brides ask people to help them put glitter on 500 tiny boxes that are filled with pink almonds. It would be a fun show to watch, because every episode would involve drug overdoses and homicide.

If you really feel like you need to hand your guests something as they are leaving, give them two doughnuts and a handful of Advil.

"Brick House"

If I hear this song again or see one more uncle break his hip to it, I'm going to pull a double Van Gogh and send my bleeding ears to the couple on their honeymoon.

(Originally appeared in a similar form on HowAboutWe)

NOT ENOUGH SYLLABLES
(a haiku for Mark Zuckerberg)

Ain't no party like

A Facebook party, 'cause a

Facebook party don't

EASY NOW

Sometimes

In a status update

I see where one of my friends has liked another friend's comment

(Even though these two people don't know each other)

And it makes me so happy

That I just want those friends to friend each other

And then friends of those friends to friend each other

And then friends of those friends' friends to friend each other

And then I think:

Whoa

Not so fast

That's how syphilis got started.

SO. YOU THINK YOU CAN DANCE?

So. You think you can dance? Huh, big guy? You really think so?

Oh, sure. I bet you can pull off a sad version of the Robot and maybe three-quarters of a Box Step. Maybe even a little Cha Cha Cha and the Y.M.C.A. And, of course, anyone with two left feet can bumble their way through the Electric Slide and the Macarena. But can you Salsa and Samba? Can you Mambo and Rumba? Can you Hora and Hornpipe? Can you T-A-N-G-O?

Oh.

I see.

Nicely done.

Well, then. How about the Lindy Hop? The Charleston? The Mashed Potato? The Carolina Shag? I bet you…

Okey doke.

Never mind.

I retract that wager.

Hmmmm. Let me think. Aha! I've got it! What about the East Coast Swing? The West Coast Swing? The Schottische? The...

REALLY?!

Wait a second.

Did you just do a pirouette while I was talking to you?

Now, looky here, Mr. Bojangles. Let me tell you a thing or two. You might entertain with your fancy dancing, but I'd like to see your version of the Cabbage Patch Kid or the Urkel. Or the Sprinkler or the Bartman. And you better believe it, no one -- and I mean NO ONE -- can do the Stanky Leg like me.

Hmph.

Except, apparently, you: The Dancing Asshole.

All I can say is, is that it looks a lot like somebody just happened to come from a very affluent background. Maybe someone used a lot of Daddy's money and a lot of Mommy's time and was fortunate enough to take years and years of private dance lessons while the rest of us kids spent our after-school hours trying to hit an acorn with a stick while our mother drank drugstore Chianti in bed and our father was off screwing the secretary of the bankrupt family wallpaper business.

Sound familiar, Fred Astaire? Sound like anybody you know? I bet this same somebody probably got white-patent-alligator-skin tap shoes for Christmas while the rest of us watched our father beat the crap out of a second-hand Atari with a steel meat tenderizer because he couldn't figure out how to put the batteries in. Never mind that an Atari doesn't even take batteries, or that the secretary showed up in her negligee for a plate of Christmas goose -- the same goose my mother ended up throwing out, pan and all, onto the frozen driveway, but not before calling my father a royal bastard-ass for all of Maple Street to hear. Never mind that, Gene Kelly. While you were tripping the light fantastic in your new pair of exorbitant tap shoes, I was drinking maraschino cherry juice and smoking inch-long menthol cigarette butts that I'd fished out of my father's ashtray. Oh, and duct-taping a joystick back together. Merry effing Christmas.

So, listen up, Baryshnikov. You might impress the masses with your prep-school versions of "Single Ladies (Put A Ring On It)" and "Crank That (Soulja Boy)," but just because you think you can dance doesn't mean you're a better person than me. Just because you can take the Nordic Polska, segue from the Cotton-Eyed Joe into the Worm, mix in a little Boot Scoot Boogie and Flamenco, and top it all off with a downpour-inducing Native

American Rain Dance/Pop 'N' Lock doesn't mean you're happier or wealthier or will never need a hair transplant or are 67 percent less likely to suffer a heart attack than those of us who've been rendered impotent by a poorly executed Moonwalk attempt.

Oh, who am I kidding?

Of course it does.

Compared to your Algorithm March, my sophomoric Hand Jive looks like a distress signal.

So, before you go -- off to wow the women with a Headspin and the Bolero -- if it's not too much of an imposition, can I ask you one final thing?

May I have this dance?

(Originally appeared in a similar form on The Big Jewel)

I DON'T KNOW. A SORORITY MAYBE?

Mommy?

Yes

Are you whistling the Mickey Mouse Clubhouse song?

No. The Harlem Globetrotters theme

Oh........Who are the Harlem Blowjobbers?

I JUST WANT PEOPLE TO KNOW I'M WINNING THE LOWEST EXPECTATIONS CONTEST

I didn't think the day could get

Any better

But I just found a pair of $3 aviators

And infant acetaminophen suppositories

At Walmart

WHEN I WAS YOUR AGE:
BEACH VACATION EDITION

Child: Waaah!!! We're not driving in a 4G network, so I can't download a new app!! Waaaah!!

Parent: What?! What did you just say? Did you just pour verbal kerosene into my ear canal? Because when I was your age, we didn't have iPads or iPhones or 4G networks. Much less, minivans with DVD players and air conditioning. No, sir. When I was your age, we rode all the way to Florida in a combustible Ford Pinto with nothing more than a book of Polish word finds for entertainment. And when we stopped to eat something, it was roadkill. So, suck it up, Nellie Oleson!! Or I'm gonna hand you half a possum and a Portuguese-to-English-to-Portuguese dictionary.

Child: HEY!! You got sunscreen in my eye!!!!

Parent: Sunscreen? SUNSCREEN? Do you know how lucky you are to EVEN HAVE SUNSCREEN? Because when I was your age, they didn't have SUNSCREEN. They only had SPF -75 crude oil and children were left to blister like neglected sausages on the beach while the adults had key parties. It WAS the 70s, for godsakes. That's what grown ups DID. They went out and got oral gonorrhea while their children contracted skin cancer.

Child: Why don't they have the Sprout Channel in this dumb condo?

Parent: Here. Enjoy what I enjoyed as a child: a Betamax tape of Jimmy Carter speeches.

Child: Ouch! I don't like how this sand feeeeels.

Parent: You don't say. Well, do you see any goddamned syringes? Because when I was your age, the beaches from Perth to Prince Edward Island were littered with syringes. One time, I even overdosed on heroin just flipping over to even out my tan.

Child: I'm bored. I don't have anything to DO on vacation.

Parent: Well, thank your lucky stars, King Toot. Because when I was your age and on vacation, that's all we had: STUFF TO DO. We had to empty cigarette butts out of poorly-designed, wicker trash baskets. We had to stand on the television, wrapped in aluminum foil like human antennae, so our parents could watch hostages die. We had to squeeze vodka from a conch shell so the lifeguards wouldn't molest us. And when we didn't have anything to do? We just had to sit. In a horrible Sears beanbag chair in some rental unit and think about Communists while our melanoma progressed. So, enjoy your boredom, little fella. Or I might just have to help you build the most amazing sandcastle ever.

Child: When can we go to Disney World? I wanna go to Disney World!

Parent: When I was your age, Disney World wasn't Epcot and Animal Kingdom and Hollywood Studios and Typhoon Lagoon and Blizzard Beach and Downtown Disney and Disney's BoardWalk and the ESPN Funtastic Fartzone. No. All it was was the Magic Kingdom. And when I was your age, the Magic Kingdom was just the "It's a Small World" ride. And it just so happened that when I finally got to go to the Magic Kingdom, the "It's a Small World" ride was under construction and the only thing open in the whole park was the wheelchair rental. So, that's all I got to do when I went to Disney World: rent a wheelchair.

Child: This dragon pool float is stupid.

Parent: Well, it's better than Styrofoam packing peanuts isn't it? Because when I was your age, that's what our parents shoved down our bathing suits to keep us afloat.

Child: I don't believe you.

Parent: You're right. I lied. We rode on corpses. Dead, bloated bodies. And sometimes they were even people we knew -- if we were lucky, that is. Now. Go get your gold-plated binoculars. It's time for you to sit on the balcony while I collect seashells for you so your hands don't get sandy.

ON THE BRIGHT SIDE

I was driving along just now

And happened to see

A blind man

Walking down the sidewalk

And holding one of those long, flexible canes in one hand

And a 36-pack of Charmin in the other

He obviously had no idea how this made him look

WHAT A WASTE OF GOOD SARCASM

Son? What did you have for lunch today?

Sweet Beef!

Did that come with a side of Cool Beans?

No. They were warm.

ALMOST-TRUE OLYMPIC BACKSTORIES

Bits of things I could have sworn I overheard commentators say during London's 2012 Olympic Summer Games.

Equestrian Eventing

Here comes Dirk Fuchstein of the Netherlands. He's riding Sir Peacock's Delight, which is actually his second mount choice. His first horse, Shiny Black Hitler, was saved by his blind sister from a barn fire when Dirk was but a boy living in a non-working windmill. Unfortunately, three days before these Olympic Games, Shiny Black Hitler collapsed in his stall after choking on a turnip. So, here Dirk is on a rather homely chestnut gelding that, ohhhhhhh. Ohhh my. What a shame. He's just crashed through an Elton John-shaped water feature. That's going to cause Dirk to lose at least eight-tenths of a point, if not both of his legs. For what it's worth, did you know these cross-country jumps were handcrafted by a Welsh boys' choir? Yes. Yes, they were. I think they were paid in jeans shorts.

Synchronized Diving

This mildly overweight duo likes to collect rubber duckies when they're not finishing each other's sentences. It's really amazing to watch their technique. It's almost like something from a slumber party routine. But really, it's a good thing they've made it to the Olympics. Their dream of the gold almost died in a Heathrow gift shop when they couldn't find matching Tinkerbell keychains. Another Cinderella story, I tell you. Way to go, Donna and Shonna.

Table Tennis

Did you just see the way that guy served? God save the queen, am I watching an Olympic sport or are we seeing video footage from an insane asylum's recreation room security camera? What? I've got the official word. We ARE watching video footage from an insane asylums's recreation room security camera.

Water Polo

This Russian team is truly amazing. They've been through quite a lot together in the past year, including but not limited to: six plane crashes, 87 prostitutes, and an appearance at the Nickelodeon Kids' Choice Awards. They're known for their very regimented style of play that's punctuated by binge drinking. Two months ago, a team-wide bout of leprosy almost left them short-handed. It's interesting to note that Olympic officials have upped the amount of chlorine in the pool today. Here's a final fun fact: Russian Dressing has less pickle relish than Thousand Island and most Russians will bite your nose off for a nickel.

Gymnastics

Riddle me this: how many barrettes does it take to hold up one anemic Polish gymnast's pitiful ponytail? The answer is 47, two cans of glitter Aqua Net, and a blood transfusion. Did you know the vault was invented in Athens in 300 B.C. when a short man escaped death by lion by jumping over a water buffalo? Speaking of buffalo wings, where can I get some more pot?

Beach Volleyball

These are the hottest people on the planet. Did I tell you that, thanks to them, I'm now bisexual? Also, that Venezuelan fellow there, the one with the asscheeks that could unscrew an eyeglass screw? He is sponsored by Nike and has an inoperable brain tumor. Now, back to Women's Weightlifting.

WANNA GO GET MANI/PEDIS, FLUFFY?

My son says he won't get married when he grows up
That's too bad, I say
You might get lonely

No, he says
I won't
I can eat dinner with my cat

This is depressing on many levels
But mostly because
I didn't plan on taking up cigarillos at age 70
And commiserating in the kitchen
With what will likely be a Manx

PHRASES COMMONLY USED BY 1950's HOUSEWIVES THAT WERE OFTEN MISINTERPRETED BY THE HOUSEWIVES' HUSBANDS AS BLATANT REQUESTS FOR SEX

"I think it's time to wax the linoleum."

"Has anyone seen my muffin pan?"

"Looks like I forgot to pay the milkman."

"I'll just put my pie on the windowsill to cool."

"How about brown-bagging it for lunch tomorrow, Dear?"

"Yahtzee!"

"Ward, it's time you and the Beaver had a little chat."

(Originally appeared in a similar form on McSweeney's Internet Tendency)

NO. NO. A THOUSAND TIMES NO.

Hey. You. Yes, you. The one in the parachute pants.

You need to stop saying "yes" and start saying "no."

How do I know? Well, for starters, you have way too many encyclopedias, stray cats, and sexually transmitted diseases for someone who knows how to politely decline.

Not to mention. You're using a Shake Weight.

Now. Why don't you put that down and lend me an ear? I promise it'll be one of the last times you say "yes."

So. Here we are in a restaurant. Not a real restaurant, per se, but my own little pretend one: The No Cafe. Everything I ask you here at The No Cafe should be answered with a "no." Except for the following question: Understand?

Good. Let's begin.

Would you like to hear our specials?
Can I get you something to start?
Breadstick?
Fresh ground pepper?

Wine list?

Tap water?

Are we good over here?

You still workin' on that?

How about a go-box?

All set?

I'm sorry. Do you have something other than American Express?

Wonderful! What a nice succession of "nos" you provided.
You're fast becoming a pro at no!

Now. Let's move on to our second lesson: Different Ways To Say
"No" Other Than "No." First, I'll rattle off a litany of questions.
Then I'll follow with a number of ways to answer in the negative.

Here we go:

Do you prefer the window seat? Would you like that on the
rocks? Does this smell funny to you? Did you hug your dog
today? Are you voting for Nader? Is canned ham an appropriate
hostess gift? Cocaine? Argyle? May I touch your monkey? Will
you be visiting our gift shop? How about a slice of pie? Less
cowbell? Virginia Slim? Can you spare a dime?

And here's how you should answer:

Nope. Nah. Nuh-uh. Most certainly not. Not on your life. No way Jose. What in the name of Satan are you thinking? Ixnay. Never. What do I look like? A goddamned idiot? Who do you think you're talking to? Oh golly, I wish I could but I can't. Eat shit. Go to hell.

Wow! You're doing great! I've almost cured you and we're almost done. But before we part ways, I'd like to remind of you of: The Things To Always, No Matter What, Say "No" To. These include:

Sierra Mist Free.
Yentl.
A two-legged cat.
Crotchless thongs.
Peach-flavored cigars.
One more spin around the dance floor.
Co-signing.
A weekend in Toledo.
Hominy.
Bill Paxton.
Watersports.
Quahogs that have been sitting out in the sun way too long.

So, there! Easy enough! I think you've passed the class! From here on out, you'll be free from commitment and regret. No more fundraiser gift wrap. No more "running buddies." No more emptying the neighbors' litter box while they're away for the winter in Siesta Key. It's just you and your "no" for the rest of eternity.

Except, of course, for those two little things we always say "yes" to:

Johhny Depp and Percocet.

I'M NOT GONNA LIE.
I WAS SCARED TO GUESS AND BE WRONG

Last night
My husband and I
Got into a cab
And the driver immediately started banging
On the ceiling light with his fist
Turning it off and on

"Welcome to Kentucky Cash Cab!!!"
He screamed in a Middle Eastern accent
"Question number one: Name the capital of Jordan!!!!!"

I like to think of myself as a geography buff
But after an undisclosed amount of cocktails
I could not come up with this at all

(FYI: Springfield is usually a decent guess
But not in this instance)

CONDITIONAL LOVE

I've reached Rite Aid's

Platinum Level

And have qualified for a 10%-off shopping spree

Which does not include:

Prescription drugs

Cigarettes

Alcohol

Lottery tickets

Money orders

Or stamps

So

What you're saying

Rite Aid

Is that you love me

But you want me to change?

I DID IT ALL FOR THE NOOK-Y

One of the lovely perks of a long-term relationship is that sleeping together stops meaning "having sex" and starts meaning "seeing one another in long johns and Clearasil." It also involves deciphering and respecting one another's bedtime routine -- a most sacred rigmarole that can include pillow fluffing, mouthwash gargling, nose spraying, alarm-clock setting, and wrinkle creaming. Or that horribly disruptive process of book reading.

You think reading a book is a quiet pursuit? I beg to differ. Because on the cusp of waking and sleeping, there's a foggy state of consciousness where even benign noises are obnoxiously amplified. Your chiming text alert becomes a gong; a baby's sigh a nor'easter; and your significant other's turning of a book page the milling and paving of an airport tarmac.

"Who just razed a skyscraper?!?!" I've been known to shout, while bolting upright in bed and removing my bite guard. "Did the hand of Goliath just scrape away the crust of the earth?!?!"

"Geez," my husband replies. "I'm just reading."

"Well, can you please read QUIETER?"

It's requests as such that keep neighborhood bars in business.

But anyway. THOSE BOOKS. With all their damn page-turning noise. Not to mention the blinding, unforgivable miner's headlamp that my husband uses to read his ear-splitting literature. It's a duo set on destroying my sleep and sanity, second only to my two sons. So recently, after a particularly crinkly biography and a new miner's bulb that apparently came straight from an Autobahn headlight, I did something I swore I'd never do: I downloaded a book onto our iPad.

As a lover of books (What? Did I make it sound like I felt otherwise?), this was tantamount to shredding a first-edition copy of *A Confederacy of Dunces* and using it as hamster bedding. However, once that cute little book icon showed up on the screen, with its silent pages illuminated by a glow that can only be called "lullaby blue," I was a convert. My husband was now free to improve his intellect by reading *The Best of Thoroughbred Handicapping*, while I drifted off to dreamland uninterrupted.

So, here's a couple of odes to e-readers. A haiku and a limerick professing my love:

Sweet, silent e-book
Couple's counselor disguised
And much, much cheaper.

What's worse to bring into bed:

A hooker or book to be read?

Some say the whore,

But unless she's a snorer,

The book is the one you should dread.

So, thank you, all-things Kindle-like for making my bedtime conflict-free. And thanks to my husband for agreeing to read QUIETER. (Also. You may wonder what I am doing on my side of the bed to make our nightlife more delightful. Well, for starters, I've switched to a flesh-colored zit cream.)

(Originally appeared in a similar form on The Huffington Post and HowAboutWe)

THE SADDEST EMAIL IN THE WHOLE WORLD

Hello, Whitney M. Collins

Amazon.com recommends

"Angry Birds Sterile Bandages"

A TEACHING MOMENT

The educational value
Of a hamster
Should not be underestimated

I think
The most lasting lesson for my children
Will be that it's not just acceptable
But preferable
To sleep in a pile of one's feces

MMMMMM. LARD TARTS.

I'm watching Paula Deen right now

I think it's the episode where she got diabetes.

UNDERREPORTED BERMUDA TRIANGLE STORIES

We were on a commuter flight from Fort Pierce, Florida to Nassau. Halfway there, the plane lost cabin pressure and from my vantage point in Seat 8C, the clouds outside appeared almost lilac in appearance. Not lavender, mind you. Lilac. A few minutes later, the flight attendant stopped in our aisle to ask us to put on our oxygen masks. It was then that I realized she was actually Cheryl Harmon -- my freshman year roommate from Utah State! Talk about uncanny! We briefly hugged and cried and exchanged email addresses before the cabin regained pressure. When no one was looking, Cheryl gave me two extra packs of peanuts -- which came in handy once we landed because our airport shuttle was late and my blood sugar dipped way low. Coincidence? I think not.
-- Sandy K., Provo, UT

My wife Tanya and I were deep sea fishing near the Turks and Caicos when she, who HATES fishing, caught a record-breaking dusky grouper. I, on the other hand, caught a cold. Also, our fishing guide looked like Bigfoot.
-- Bill S., Chattanooga, TN

As a Coast Guard officer, I see lots of strange things in the Bermuda Triangle. But nothing was as weird as that guy I

rescued off the coast of Miami who had four nipples. Three? I could maybe handle that. But four? I can't even talk about it.
-- Frank W., Coral Gables, FL

I was on a Carnival Cruise with a bunch of my bros en route to San Juan. I swear, one night by the upper deck pool, I was probed by aliens. It was definitely the same night my frat brothers and I took mescaline. Or maybe it was the Purple Hooch night. Whatever the case, the next morning, my ass hurt. I hate the Bermuda Triangle. But Puerto Rico was pretty cool.
-- Josh G., Austin, TX

My husband and I were in Bimini and he put his dirty dishes in the dishwasher. I repeat: my husband put his dirty dishes INSIDE the dishwasher. Not to mention, my 16-year-old daughter laughed at a knock-knock joke. God help us all. It's only a matter of time before the entire planet is sucked into a wormhole.
-- Helen F., Trenton, NJ

Some people say Key West is not included in the Bermuda Triangle. Well, you know what I say to that? They're idiots who have obviously never seen Dominique and his Flying Housecats at the Westin Pier's Sunset Celebration.
-- Bruce D., Milwaukee, WI

I got really really lost while sightseeing in Jamaica. I mean wicked disoriented. I'd just bought a massive bag of Negril sinsemilla when my inner compass just went totally wack. I also think I saw those aliens who violated Josh. Anyway, the only way I was able to finally get back to the condo was to travel through the lost city of Atlantis, hug four palm trees, forgive my father, and eat a crapload of Cheetos.

-- Hugh C., Boston, MA

My wife and I were at a Sandals Resort in Antigua, after the birth of our triplets, when the weirdest thing happened to us during a snorkeling excursion. A methane hydrate completely stripped us of our clothes and wedding rings, minutes before a rogue wave deposited us smack in the middle of a raging swingers party. I used to be a skeptic, but after 18 sexless months and learning more about the surface velocity of the Gulf Stream, I believe pretty much anything can happen in the Bermuda Triangle. Or in Room 402.

-- Tom Q., St. Louis, MO

(Originally appeared in a similar form on The Big Jewel)

I SERIOUSLY MAY NEVER BE ABLE TO SLEEP AGAIN

How do you make a possessive possessive?

Such as

The Applebee's's salad sucked

The problem is Applebee's comes pre-apostrophed

I mean it's a singular noun

So does that mean if there are several Applebee'ses

And we're talking about multiple salads

Would it be

The Applebee'ses's salads sucked?

(I claim to be a grammar guru, but I'm not gonna lay to you. I have no idea how to use the many forms of "lie" in a sentence.)

(I'm also not gonna lain to you about this: I used to think Dire Straits was a person.)

I'M APPLYING FOR A PATENT

Instead of jeans that feel like pajamas
I'm inventing pajamas that feel like jeans
They're called Jeans Pajamas

The people in my infomercial
Are horribly uncomfortable
But they're very productive
They play fewer video games
They cry a lot
And they vote for the Communist Party

SIMILAC ALIMENTUM ADVANCE

Last Sunday morning, on the verge of both a drive-thru divorce and trading our infant son on eBay for a box of steel condoms, my husband and I invested in a foul-smelling product known as Similac Alimentum Advance, a formula made specifically for babies who, for reasons of severe protein sensitivity, begin to make Linda Blair look like Laura Ingalls. Never mind that it costs more than what was going to be our child's liberal arts education, or that it smells like 42-day-old tofu with a dash of diaper, or that I ran four red lights and gave a cop the finger while screeching toward Rite Aid. This beverage is "Buddha in a Bottle."

Immediately after his first five-ounce feeding, George's screams subsided and he slipped into an open-eyed state of nirvana, farted twice, and gave a harmonious coo. Then he slept for four hours straight, during which time my husband and I were so overcome with glee we didn't even worry about checking the baby's pulse. Today is Wednesday, and, $30 later (yes, dear readers, the price is that exorbitant), the Collins family is auditioning for Hallmark, Pillsbury, and Disney World commercials. We're that disgustingly happy.

Oh, did I mention that the proteins in Similac Alimentum Advance are pre-digested? I don't know who does that at the factory, or what it entails, but we don't give a crap. (Except for George. He's giving lots and lots of them.)

(Originally appeared in a similar form on McSweeney's Internet Tendency)

LET'S START WITH CHESS TEAM

Mommy!!! What are those men doing on TV?

They are Navy Seals.

I want to be a Navy Seal when I grow up.

That's a noble aspiration, son. They are among the strongest, most admirable people in the...

AGHGHGHGHGHGHGHGHGGHH!!!!!!!!!!! MY TONGUE, MOMMY!!!!!! I BIT MY TONGUE!!! AGHGHGHGHGHHGHGHGHGHGGH!!!!!

DID THIS COME IN THE HOOTERS HAPPY MEAL?

I just spent 45 minutes

On an Indiana Jones puzzle

43 of which were

Unfortunately devoted to finding

Shia LaBeouf's goatee

Wait

This isn't an Indy puzzle

And that's not a goatee

MY FELLOW AMERICANS,
I AM RUNNING FOR SENATE

Ladies and Gentlemen, Friends and Supporters:

It is with great pleasure that I announce my candidacy for the United States Senate. I can think of no higher honor than serving the wonderful citizens of this wonderful nation. Therefore, I'd like to take this opportunity to not only set forth my vision for this fine country of ours and to thank you for your time, but to also to beat my competitors to the punch by clearing the air over any incidents in my life that may or may not be perceived as controversial.

Firstly, if elected, I will strive to enact broader tax cuts for the hard-working middle class. I will labor hand-in-hand with both Republicans and Democrats to ensure this much-needed tax relief happens in a timely and bipartisan manner. Also, I once had a teeny-tiny DUI.

Secondly, there is nothing more grand and beautiful than our natural resources, so it goes without saying that the environment is also of utmost importance to me. Though cap-and-trade is a hotly debated topic, I'd like to move forward with stricter control of emissions, aggressive research of alternative energies, and let's go on and make that three teeny-tiny DUIs.

Universal health care is another issue I am passionate about. I'll work day and night to make it impossible for big health care to deny someone coverage because of a preexisting condition, and to also ensure single moms and kids get the help they deserve. Furthermore, believe me when I say I never, EVER beat my wife (just my girlfriend) and man that heroin looks delicious!

While we're on the topic of drugs, I'm adamant about securing our borders to prevent any increase in the illegal drug trade. There's nothing worse than subjecting our precious children, America's future, to addictive substances. Nothing worse. Except maybe for having sex a donkey, which I've been known to do from time to time. Donkeys and pugs.

So, in conclusion: let's build some highways, let's revamp No Child Left Behind, I think life begins at conception, where can I get some cheap cock, whose dildo is this on the podium, I'm wearing ladies' underwear, let's build lots of mosques at Ground Zero, I don't know how I feel about Israel, I like breast implants on men, the government should pay for hair plugs, and one time I pooped on a moving escalator.

Thank you for your vote.

LET'S JUST GET IT ALL DONE AT ONCE

How much does a facelift cost?

How about a mini one?

What about a mini lift and a neck lift combo?

Does that include getting your eyes done?

What would it cost to add on some Botox?

How about some laser stuff?

And maybe a peel?

What are these filler things?

HOW MUCH?

Oh

Never mind

What do you charge for decapitation?

DO YOUR JEANS HAVE A ZIPPER
THE SIZE OF A RAILROAD TRACK?

When I see someone wearing
One of those Polo shirts
With the GIANT polo player on it
I have this pretend conversation in my head:

Me: Hey, pardon me. There's something on your shirt.

Idiot: What? Oh. That's a giant polo player.

Me: Well, thank goodness. I thought it was a gunshot wound/
vomit/a massive birthmark peeking through a huge ripped hole
and not a status symbol. By the way, when did Ralph Lauren
totally lose his shit?

Idiot: Nice talking to you.

AN OAKEN NUGGET FOR ME LUVE

I suppose at some point in history, it was considered sensible and sexy to acknowledge the thirteenth year of marriage with a doily. Because on the list of traditional anniversary gifts, that's what's recommended as a gift for people who've spent more than a DECADE listening to one another slurp soup: LACE.

Now, I don't know about you, but when I've spent close to 15 YEARS finding someone else's fingernail clippings in my car cup holder, I'm going to expect something more than a tatted handkerchief that requires hand-washing in Woolite.

Furthermore, in addition to not only believing it's unrealistic to give a couple DESK SETS for their seven-year itch, I also believe it's unrealistic to think most contemporary twosomes will wait until years of coupledom have passed to celebrate their union in grand fashion.

So, here are seven relationship milestones that deserve both recognition and gifts (also known as a fine opportunity for me to throw some of the standard anniversary suggestions under the bus).

Changing Your Relationship Status

For most modern couples, declaring you're "In A Relationship" on Facebook is a decision that involves (or should involve) a fair amount of contemplation. In fact, the olden day equivalent of this milestone is a full year of arranged marriage, for which the traditionalists suggest a First Anniversary gift of…PAPER.

WHAT?! Congratulations on telling 600 of your closest friends you are no longer on the market! Here's a little something from the coffee filter family! Nope. I think I'll pass. This one deserves bacon. Thick-cut and peppered.

Attending Your Mate's High School Reunion

Typically, this event involves plenty of other people's alcohol poisoning and hip fractures, so any initial awkwardness on your part should quickly dissipate. But, it can be a watershed moment in a relationship -- one where folks finally prove to the former class president that they haven't been lying about their girlfriend.

So, some sort of gift that honors your significant other's ability for small talk is in order. Perhaps the recommended Second Anniversary present of cotton? Because doing body shots with your drunk track coach earned me some gauze, and feigning interest in your old locker combination earned me some tube socks, and getting a concussion on the dance floor, courtesy of your ex-girlfriend's massive tits, most definitely earned me a king set of 1500-thread count Egyptian cotton sheets.

Meeting The Parents

There have been entire trilogies of bad movies based on this exact premise, because it's usually on par with a public pap smear. Anything that requires an entire weekend of not pooping and not mentioning you majored in puppeteering deserves a reward.

We could go with the Third Anniversary of leather for this benchmark, but I'm letting you know right now that a Western saddle isn't going to make up for your stepfather complimenting "my hindquarters" unless that saddle is attached to Pegasus. So, let's try concert tickets. And by "concert" I mean "gold" and by "tickets" I mean "necklace."

Moving In Together

This is HUGE. Or not. It really depends on how much rent it costs for a one-bedroom in the city where you live. Regardless, cohabitation does earn a place on the relationship timeline. So, let's nod at this one with the Sixth Anniversary gift of candy. A King Size bag of Skittles should suffice. I mean, I can't think of anything better than a handful of fruit chews in exchange for agreeing to let your man hang that Icehouse beach towel instead of curtains.

Planning A Wedding

I'm not going to lie. Planning a wedding was one of the most stressful things I've ever done. How do we NOT invite those people? Will so-and-so's complexion look good in navy? What if the onion tartlets are more like mini quiches? Can we play that song on a loudspeaker during the champagne toast thingy? And where for the love of Vera Goddamned Wang can I get a cake knife shaped like AN OSTRICH FEATHER?!?!

Suffice it to say, even the most mellow tomboy-of-a-girl will, at some point during this preparatory hell, contemplate throwing herself off an overpass, because she will probably yell "I SPECIFICALLY SAID SPEARMINT AND NOT CELADON!" at a priest.

So, to laud the groom in question here, I'm going to recommend the 35th Anniversary gifts of coral and jade.

(And Coral and Jade are hookers.)

Birth Of A Child

Some of you may choose to solidify (or greatly stress) your union by making a baby. This baby will, like it or not, destroy at least one reproductive system, empty your bank account, scream during *Mad Men*, and eventually steal all your liquor.

A gift exchange is ABSOLUTELY in order for this achievement. Might I suggest the 80th Anniversary gift of oak? Because I just found a fucking acorn. Not a walnut, mind you. Not a pinecone. AN ACORN. Here. Take it. I INSIST. HERE'S TO NEVER SLEEPING AGAIN, ENJOY THIS OAKEN NUGGET.

Just kidding. This accomplishment calls for big stuff. He should get a Porsche and she should get a boob job, both of which are paid for with the child's college fund.

Making Out A Will

This is a landmark moment. This is where you sit down in a lawyer's office and discuss horrible things, like: Who will raise our children if we die? How much money will you leave me if you get hit by a bus, because all I'm qualified to do is tweet? And, most importantly, do you prefer a feeding tube or for me to just yank the ever-loving shit out of the plug?

Stuff like this will make you laugh and cry and reach for an Emily Post book for gift advice, because surely the pinnacle of suggested anniversary presents will make you feel better about your slow, painful, pending deaths.

What's that? The 90th ANNIVERSARY gift suggestion is STONE? Because after 90 YEARS of smelling your man's dutch ovens, here's a stone?! Because nothing is cuter than first grade sweethearts who've shared the same toilet for the lifespan of a giant tortoise, so here's a piece of gravel? So, how 'bout this? Let's go on and make that stone my HEADSTONE.

And now we know how the WWII generation stayed together so long: it's because they had absolutely NO ROMANTIC EXPECTATIONS whatsoever.

Anyway. Back to that will. You just made out a depressing legal document, and I was going to suggest a trip to Key West to acknowledge this special and difficult event. But thanks to those Depression-era people, I guess we'll now just settle for an apple cobbler Yankee Candle and a shared Pabst. Cheers, Baby. You better leave me your grandmother's sterling shot glasses.

(Originally appeared in a similar form on HowAboutWe)

WHEN YOU GET A CHANCE, CAN I GET
TWO STEEL BREAD KNIVES FOR MY EARDRUMS?

HI THERE!!!!!!!! MY NAME IS SHANNON!!!!!! WELCOME
TO PANERA!!!!!!!! DO YOU HAVE YOUR "MY PANERA"
CARD?!?!?!??!?!?!!?!?!?

(15 minutes later after dumping an entire Lactaid/tampon/
magnifying readers factory out of my purse and onto the floor of
Panera)

WOW!!!!!! IT LOOKS LIKE THIS CARD WAS NEVER
ACTIVATED!!!!!!!!! YOU'LL NEED TO GO ONLINE WHEN
YOU GET HOME AND ACTIVATE YOUR CARD. IT'S
REALLY SUPER EASY!!!!!!!!!!

Tell you what, Shannon. Why don't you be a dear and put those
onion bagels in a separate bag from the cinnamon bagels then
take my engagement ring and pawn it and use the money to have
your voicebox surgically removed?

AT KROGER'S

I was just at the grocery late-night

To buy Brussels sprouts

And in the parking lot

A teenage couple was making out on the hood of a car

And inside

An old couple was holding hands and saying

Why do they never have those limas anymore?

Which limas?

You know. The little limas.

And then I said to myself

There is a poem here

And I shall title it: Pork and Beans

DRESS CODES DEMYSTIFIED

Black Tie (aka Formal)
Yes: Black tuxedo jackets and matching trousers, patent leather shoes for men. Evening gowns or cocktail dresses for women. No: Khakis, nose rings.

Black Tie Optional (aka Semi-formal, Indecisive, Passive-aggressive)
Tuxedos or dark suits for men. Evening gowns or cocktail dresses for women. Pantyhose or no pantyhose. Top hat or no top hat. Attend or don't attend. See if I care. Not that you'd care if I cared. I may not even go myself. I might have something better to do. But if I do end up going, I'll probably have a sinus infection. Or cancer.

White Tie (aka Ultra-formal)
Pretty much the same as Black Tie. Except racist.

Texas Black Tie
Pretty much the same as White Tie. Except homophobic. Oh…and spurs.

Executive
Orange jumpsuit, handcuffs, Gucci loafers.

Smart Casual vs. Business Casual
Blue jeans and bifocals vs. Banana slings and ballpoints.

Casual Friday
Dockers, bed heads, Birkenstocks, mild cases of chlamydia.
(Casual Friday is not to be confused with Lackadaisical
Wednesday, which permits flip flops and gonorrhea; or Devil-
May-Care Tuesday, which authorizes Crocs and crabs. Please
note: cutoffs, snoods, gladiator sandals, and genital warts are
solely reserved for Manic-Depressive Thursday. We do not care
what you wear on Suicidal Sunday, but keep in mind, a little
rouge never looked bad on anyone.)

Festive (aka Holiday, Humiliating)
Yes: Sequins, musical neckties, tap shoes, dickies, clown noses,
Groucho Marx glasses.
No: Recollection of how you ended up behind the office copy
machine spooning with a Chia Pet.

Rugged (aka Sporting, Lesbian)
Yes: Orvis, pelts, slingshots.
No: Spandex, leg warmers, deodorant.

Resort (aka Cruise, Water Park)
Yes: Disney attire, fanny packs, cellulite, Aqua Socks, body hair,
suspicious moles, moose knuckles.

No: Concealed weapons, open wounds, Ph.D.s, dignity.

After Five

Yes: Sweatpants, preferably velour. Terry cloth. Red Lobster bibs. Zit cream.

No: I do not want to get back together with you. I just stopped by to get my DVDs and toothbrush. What's that? I can't have them until I have sex with you? Hmm. Let me sit here on the couch and think about that. Meanwhile, why don't you go get me a beer while I finish your lobster? And a glass. A frosty one.

Mardi Gras (see also: Nursing Home, Nursery School)

No: Bras.

Yes: Diapers.

Dressy Casual

Pair an "A" item with a "B" item.

A: Wife beater, overalls, corncob pipe, trucker hat.

B: Tweed knickers, hoop skirt, cummerbund, monocle.

Rehearsal Dinner

Dude! Screw the rented tux; all you're gonna need is a paper bag for your head. I am so totally going to bring up that time when we did that thing. And that other time when we did that other thing. If I get on a roll, I may even mention those two other times and those two other things! I am so going to make you hate me, and your fiancee hate you! It'll be awesome, Bro! I'm also going to pick up half of my pork tenderloin during the speech and waggle it between my legs to illustrate a point. Then I'll shed a few tears before grabbing your grandmother's ass at the open bar. Soon after, I'll puke. Any chance I can have your paper bag?

Country Club
Yes: J.Crew "critter" pants, ballet flats, tortoiseshell accessories, alcoholics (non-recovering).
No: Cosby sweaters, Drakkar Noir, Discover cards, Mormons.

Catholic School
Yes: Kilts, hemmed four inches higher than catalog standard. Dime bag in kneesocks. Cigarettes in padded bra. General countenance of ennui.
No: Fishnets. Yarmulkes. Mohawks. Ass-less chaps. Pasties. Pearl necklaces. Chewing gum in confession, Missy.

Le Smoking
Yes: This is an actual dress code.
No: I didn't make it up.
Suggestions: Wear a beret. Drive your Le Car. Shave your le balls. Plan on doing lots of le cocaine.

Midwestern Thanksgiving Dinner

No: Bare feet, slouching, death metal concert tees, low-rise jeans, hickeys, Methodist jokes, tattoos, scatological humor, mini skirts, eyeliner, eye rolling, Doc Martens, wallet chains, Hannah Montana paraphernalia, or, God forbid, that vulgar v-neck number. What happened to that Lands' End turtleneck we sent you last Christmas? Don't tell me you gave it away. It's probably all because of that man you're co-habitating with. Oh, mother of pearl...the yams!

Yes: Horse tranquilizers, Snuggie.

(Originally appeared in a similar form on The Big Jewel)

GOODNIGHT, COCKROACH

Once

When I was reading the children a bedtime story

Out of nowhere

There was a massive beetle

Crawling on my neck

Which turned storytime

Into a valuable teaching moment

Of when it's OK to say

(Or even scream)

SUCK IT, GRANDMA!!!

SO MANY HORRIBLE THINGS IN THIS WORLD

Floods

Hurricanes

Earthquakes

Famine

Nuclear weapons

Aligning printer cartridges

THE SPAWN OF IGGY POP'S ASSHOLE

When cats stare at you, in addition to incinerating your inferior soul, they're saying one of five things in a British accent: "Has anyone seen my monocle?" "Friskies? Surely you jest." "I did God's will and urinated on your resume." "Time to sift my feces!" And: "You really should consider killing yourself." It's amazing kittens grow into cats, because all kittens say is: "Hep! Hep! Me so tiny! Hep! Hep me, pweeze!" Then they do a little shaky stumble into a wall like they're blind and hypothermic, and you're suddenly willing to breastfeed them.

So, when I was asked a few summers ago if I knew someone who might be willing to gather 12 abandoned kittens from a barn and either find them homes/take them to the rescue center, I said: "OH, DO I!"

Because I am a moron.

Do you know how to catch 12 kittens? Here's a hint: It's not with a telescoping dust mop and a saucer of pretzel rods. Because even though that seems like the most logical approach, kittens catch on quick. The first two will innocently crawl up your leg and start suckling one of your jeans' rivets, but the next 10 will morph into cockroaches on meth who apparently don't like Rold Gold. Trust me on this.

Also? Have you ever seen ugly kittens? Well, word to your mother, there is nothing more terrifying than an animal that looks like the spawn of Iggy Pop's asshole. These felines I encountered were a hissing, diseased, rabid batch of mottled rats that can only be described as Satan's fur turds. Four of them carried switchblades and Hepatitis C, three of them smoked Luckys, and two of them had testicles instead of eyes. In short, these weren't your calendar cats. Not a-one of them could've graced a Scholastic book order poster -- unless it was a poster for dysentery awareness.

Anyway, in case you're interested, here's what I named them during the three hours it took me to dust-mop them into laundry baskets held together with painters' tape: Pus in Boots, Little Cysty, Ether Face, Mr. Herpes, Kornshit, Staphanie, Bleeding Anus, Coach K, Toilet Clog, Aiden, Jaden, and Jesus Wept.

After four asthma attacks and a sneezing fit that caused a brain hemorrhage, I finally got that massive crackbasket of calico kidney stones into my truck. It was like carpooling with Medusa's head. I took a photo of the kittens and posted it to Facebook to see if anyone wanted to adopt, but all 500 of my friends promptly unfriended me before immersing their heads in buckets of battery acid.

So, I had nowhere to take the cats but the Humane Society. When I dropped them off, I was brilliant enough to take the least ugly (I think it was Little Cysty) home to my 4-year-old son. The rest stayed with the pound lady who gave me the same look the Salvation Army folks reserve for people who drop off a few milk crates of used adult diapers.

To wrap this up a little more quickly, Little Cysty died. But not before he gave my entire family ringworm. I couldn't believe he ended up having a contagious disease, because he'd actually been somewhat attractive in dim light! But I'm sure that's what Channing Tatum's ex-girlfriends all say.

Interesting fact: ringworm isn't a worm, it's just a fungus. Just a fungus that takes about 14 months to eradicate from your carpet and scalp, using bleach, Selsun Blue, a fine tooth comb meant for eyebrows, a flamethrower, an exorcism, and holy water. In those 14 months, I got pregnant and we got my son another cat. A cat that ended up getting ringworm from a chair Little Cysty had walked past, so, we banished him to the garage. And the baby? We named him Ammonia.

When it comes to cats, there are two types of people. Those who will read this story and say: "Why didn't that bitch just shave those kittens and then apply antifungal cream to their bald bodies using her tongue like their cat mama would have?" And

there are those who will read this and say: "Why didn't that bitch put those kitties in one of those cat swimming bags? You know. The kind that's made of burlap and filled with bricks."
Regardless, when I tell this story, everyone wants me committed.

So, in summation, I only have three regrets in life: not taking that semester to Scotland, not minoring in Modern Dance, and saving those cats.

(Originally appeared in a similar form on Loop)

I THOUGHT AN ABACUS
WAS A MUSICAL INSTRUMENT

I wasn't planning on telling my children this

Until we had a neutral moderator on site

But after being asked by my oldest son today

To build both a

Working engine

And a pulley system

I think it's time I confessed

That my high school created a special math class

(For just me and a 25-year-old hockey player)

That implemented dried beans

Clap-counting

And a Hello Kitty calculator

MAYBE YOU SHOULD GET SOMEONE TO MODEL IT

My friend was an auctioneer
At a church auction
And he couldn't get anyone to bid
On a strand of cultured pearls

Hmph
Imagine that

Ladies and gentlemen!
A lovely pearl necklace!
A lovely pearl necklace!
Who wants to buy a PEARL NECKLACE?

(In public. At church.)

Please!
Someone buy this
Pearl Necklace!
God wants you to buy this
PEARL NECKLACE!

Anyone?
A PEARL NECKLACE FOR JESUS!

HOW PARENTS TALK DIRTY

"Where do you want me to stick this? In the fridge? Oh, yeah? Like this? You want me to stick this half-empty bottle of formula in the fridge before it goes bad? Watch me do it."

"How do you like it? Huh? How do you like the chili mac? Not bad, is it? Tell me it's good. Tell me. Say, 'this chili mac is so good.'"

"I've got a surprise for you. Over here. That's right. Over here in my pants. It's a car wash coupon."

"Oh, shit. It's so big. It's so goddamned big. That's the biggest shit the dog has ever taken on the dining room rug."

"How about I bend over? In my panties. That way you can put this ThermaCare HeatWrap on my lumbar region."

"Say my name. No. Say MY NAME. That's what the kennel reservation is under."

"Somebody's been really bad. Reeeallllllly bad. I think he needs a spanking. He's upstairs in time-out. I took away all his Legos, too."

"You wanna screw? Oh, you do? You want a big screw? Six big screws? Jesus. How many screws does that baby gate take?"

"Tell me where you want it. Tell me! Tell me where you want it! Tell me now, bitch! I can't hold this curtain rod up all day."

WHO KNEW THERE WERE SO MANY CLASSICS RIGHT BESIDE THE GERITOL AND CONDOMS?

At the pharmacy
They have a whole new shipment of
Migraines for Dummies

I have that same book under another title:
The Collected Works of Shakespeare

BETTER TAKE A HOT PLATE, TOO, TO MAKE
GRILLED CHEESES ALL AROUND

When a child puts a pan on his head

And runs around the kitchen

Screaming

"Follow me to Pothead Village!!!"

I say

"Um. I've been to Pothead Village

And you're going to get turned away

If you don't bring enough Snickers for everyone.

Here. Don't forget your poncho."

I'M THE ONE YOUR MOTHER WARNED YOU ABOUT

Yes. It's me. The one your mother warned you about. No, no, no. Not the guy with the tats and the Harley and the affinity for S&M. And not the aimless bass player with seven piercings, four illegitimate children, and three ex-wives. And certainly not the drunk with a hook for a hand who doesn't believe in herpes. (Though I must admit, all of them sound fascinating!) No, no, no, you silly old goose. Me! The other one she warned you about. You know, the replacement window salesman who has more breast tissue than you're comfortable with on a man and who won't let his peas touch his potatoes. The man who clings to his body pillow after a particularly riveting episode of *MythBusters* and cries himself to sleep. The man who can't get enough of key lime pie-flavored yogurt.

Back when we met four years ago, when you were probably falling hard and fast for my sad story of college humiliation (you know the one, where I wet my pants on the climbing wall during orientation), I bet your mother was doing her best to put in her two cents. She's so nice, and almost always right, but you so rarely listen. Now, here we are, and I can tell something's starting to give in this relationship. What is it my love? Is it my need to never be right? Is it the way I change my order six or seven times at the Arby's drive-thru? Is it my desire to always please you first and then insist on cuddling very, very, very tightly while I tremble in fear? Is it my Curious George waffle maker? The way I foxtrot? My addiction to Fruit Stripe gum? My year-long seasonal allergies? My psoriasis? My halitosis? My eight albino ferrets? My fear of thunderstorms? My chestnut toupee?

Wait. I know. How could I have not guessed? It's probably my obnoxiously huge penis.

It's probably bad enough that I insist on Donald Duck-themed checks and my grilled cheese cut into triangles when I treat you to your monthly dinner at Chili's. But this penis! My lord. This ridiculous fifth appendage of mine is a lot for a nice girl like you to tolerate. So, believe me, I certainly understand if you need to move on.

My sweet little lamb of delight, you deserve to be with a man who makes more than $700 a month before taxes. A man who knows how to use a charcoal grill, pump his own gas, pull off a Band-Aid without screaming, and open a beer can without using one of those little plastic opener thingies that prevents nail breakage. You deserve that. I know that. Your mother has always known that. So, listen to what we're telling you.

Don't make me beg, now. Please. Go. Marry that guy with the health benefits and chest hair -- that guy who can swim without earplugs (or just swim in general) and ride a bike without having a panic attack. Enjoy his sanely-proportioned body, his ability to tie his own shoes. I promise you'll never look back at me, the guy who owned a pair of lederhosen. The guy who stole your bath beads and had *You've Got Mail* memorized. The one who got sloppy, sobbing drunk on half a Michelob Ultra. Our time together will never haunt you. I'm the horribly boring, incredibly nice, man-with-a-massive-massive-package-who-for-some-really-strange-reason-was-REALLY-SUPER-hard-to-break-up-with.

I'm the one your mother warned you about.

IT'S LIKE A HORROR MOVIE TRAILER

You know that Peppermint Patty commercial

Where they zoom in

On some stranger's face

While they eat?

I can't figure out if

Those are ads

For blackhead removal

Or misanthropy

I GOT SO NERVOUS

What a relief

I thought the University of Phoenix

Was mad at me or something

He hadn't emailed me

In like four hours

A LETTER TO MY 4-YEAR-OLD SON'S
IMAGINARY FRIEND

Dear Talking Hot Dog,

Listen up, you freak. Stay away from my kid. You got that? Stay the hell away. I don't care that you live in a hole in the ground near our swingset and prefer turkey over ham. I don't care that you like riding next to my son on his way to and from school. And I don't care how much you like it when he buckles your tiny seatbelt and gives you a loving pat on your antlers. You are a CYCLOPS for cryin' out loud! You're a weiner with a voice! You sound not unlike something a mustachioed 1980's high school custodian would have tried to "introduce" me to after cheerleading practice.

I don't like you, Talking Hot Dog. Not one bit. So, before my son gets home, you better pack your acorn suitcase and get gone. Oh. I forgot. You're ALWAYS NAKED! You wouldn't HAVE any clothes to pack in a suitcase. YOU SICK, SAD, SORRY BASTARD. Get the hell out of my lawn before I call the goddam cops! SCRAM!

Best,
Whitney Collins

SOUNDS LIKE A FUN PLACE

In the Children's Dictionary
I just bought
From some door-to-door salesman
This is how they define the word "village"

A village is smaller than a city
And even smaller than a town
Not many people live in a village
Usually everybody knows everybody else in a village
Some villages have strange sounding names
Like "Balls Mills"

TLC's FALL LINEUP

Little People, Big Tapeworm

Scone Wars

I Didn't Even Know I Was Ugly

Born Without Bladders

Man vs. Diaper

Toddlers and Tequila

Sister Husbands

Say Yes to the Midget

Jon & Kate Burn in a Special Place in Hell

Corndog Boss

19 Kids and a Serious Black Tar Heroin Habit

Paranormal Squirrels

Who Painted the Den While I Was at the Spa With my Leper?

America's Next Top Meter Reader

Keeping Up With the Cupcake Whores

Ass Babies

CAN I GET ANYONE SOME MORE AMNESIA?

If I've learned one thing from daytime soaps

It's this

If

While you're snuggling in bed

You give your husband a stork statue

Because storks mate for life

You basically just asked

To be murdered

Oh

One more thing

Never lift a wedding veil

That's thicker than a beach towel

EIGHT DATES THAT SOUND
ROMANTIC BUT AREN'T

Picnics

Picnicking, like smallpox and wearing sandals made out of beaver gut, is something people used to endure because they had no choice. But for some reason, unlike excessive bleeding and intestinal shoes, picnicking has transformed from a hardship required of hunter-gatherers into the penultimate romantic date option. An entire industry is devoted to shatterproof wine glasses, titanium cheese slicers, water-resistant tartan, and wicker backpacks.

Have you ever worn a wicker backpack? I haven't, but I imagine it's not unlike hiking with an antique rocking chair strapped to your shoulders. "No, worries, my Darling. Just as soon as we scale this mountain, I'll take this lobster trap off my spinal cord, serve you some questionable chicken salad, and make sweet love to you on a pile of gravel and fire ants." I'm sure there are some folks out there who've had a lovely picnicking experience (such as imaginary people in Impressionist paintings), but personally, most of my eating-on-the-ground experiences have resulted in malaria and salmonella.

If you're really in the mood for combining hard salami, nature, and love, might I recommend holding hands and eating a Slim Jim at your neighborhood florist?

Ice Skating

Every time I go to a skating rink, I see a bunch of well-meaning guys who have obviously never strapped on a pair of skates, doing that herky-jerky Frankenstein walk as they try to keep up with a date who is pirouetting in a matching angora hat-scarf-mittens set. Inevitably, while she is simultaneously applying peppermint lip gloss and channeling Michelle Kwan, the boyfriend loses complete control of his ice stomp and begins what can only be described as an upright breaststroke-backstroke-breaststroke-backstroke, until he swoops about five feet up into the air and then lands, shattering his coccyx, all in the name of creative dating.

But don't let me talk you out of this; seeing someone you've known for 20 minutes end up in a body cast might be your thing.

Weddings

Wedding dates are responsible for 97.9% of break-ups, because there are so many things to fight about. Will we ever get engaged? Are you planning on writing your own vows? How long till we talk about at least moving in together? Did you roll your eyes during *Corinthians 13*? You did, didn't you?! HEY! Why didn't you bring me a drink from the bar? And the always inevitable: Oh, sweet Lord. Where are your pants?!

Here's my advice: if you have to attend a wedding together, make sure it's one featuring a bourbon tasting and flat-chested bridesmaids that are humiliated by having to carry parasols.

Sex on the Beach
I have enough trouble motivating myself to exfoliate my forehead. So, thanks but no thanks.

Couple's Massage
When I pay for a massage, I am paying someone big bucks to ram both elbows into my kidneys. They're going to say, "Is this too hard?" and I'm going to say through clenched teeth, "Is that all you got, you goddamned pansy?" This is quality time in which my spine is going to get aligned in 90 minutes. And when all is said and done, I plan on leaving looking like I got caught in a prehistoric hail storm. So, Honey, if you want to come recline next to me while I ask for the William Wallace treatment, by all means don't request Enya.

Hot Air Balloon
Another wicker basket activity? SHEESH! For what it's worth, I've done this. And if you can get over the fact that you're in a wastebasket in the sky, powered by fire and Dacron, then go for

it. But it's really no different than a date at a therapist's office where both of you discuss debilitating anxiety.

Twister
Did you know this is a board game invented by the makers of Beano?

Consuming Raw Oysters
Like I always say, if you can't find oysters, you can achieve pretty much the same thing by tossing a jaunty checked cloth on the table, lighting a bunch of candles, staring into one another's eyes, and dipping some Ex-Lax into cocktail sauce. Here's looking at your EpiPen, Kid.

(Originally appeared in a similar form on HowAboutWe)

HONESTLY? IT RUINED IT FOR ME

Every once in a while

I remember how fake

The tiger looked in The Hangover

And it bums me out

For about three or four days

HOW ABOUT WE GET IN THE HOT TUB AND I TELL YOU EVERYTHING I KNOW ABOUT COMMAS?

You know that John Cougar song

I Need a Lover That Won't Drive Me Crazy?

Well

Technically

It should be

I Need a Lover WHO Won't Drive Me Crazy

But she probably already told him that

SKILLZ

I seriously just saw a lady

Walking down the street

Being followed by two housecats

If her coat isn't made of ham

I would definitely consider her for babysitting

LESSER-KNOWN PATRON SAINTS

Saint Monica of Padua, Patron Saint of Tooth Decay

Rosy-cheeked and delightfully chubby, Saint Monica of Padua was originally a candy maker before her conversion in 358. Once a Catholic, she devoted her life to caring for street children, for whom she fashioned little red-and-white striped aprons and tri-corner hats and taught the ancient art of doughnut-making. Before being stoned to death in 364 (on allegations her sweet rolls were overtly sexual in appearance), Saint Monica opened up a coffee shop. Upon her canonization, her best friends Saint Rachel and Saint Phoebe became baristas and took over the cafe, but not before renaming it Central Pope. Rumors circulated after Saint Monica's death that she had carried on a sexual relationship with a pagan named Chandler, which the Church claimed to be a ridiculous assertion as everyone knew Chandler was gay.

Saint Hector, Patron Saint of Wednesdays

Saint Hector was a fairly humdrum soul from Damascus who was fortunate enough to run around with a rather impressive foursome -- Saint Valentine, Saint Patrick, jolly old Saint Nicholas, and Saint Halloween. Because of his connections, Hector was able to get into most any nightclub or procure front-row chariot race tickets at the last minute. He got a lot of girls because of this, but mostly because they wanted to meet his friends -- Saint Valentine, in particular. Eventually this depressed him, his foursome abandoned him, and Saint Hector succumbed to heavy drinking on week nights, specifically Wednesdays, when he'd slump his way into a tavern, drink himself silly, and sleep with anything that moved. This is where we get the term "Hump Day," though the Church contends it's because Hector had poor posture.

Saint Appollonia of Carthage, Patron Saint of Back-Up Singers
Born in North Africa to missionary parents, Saint Appollonia was a chaste and forlorn girl, interested mostly in nursing weak animals back to health -- specifically doves. At the ripe age of fourteen, a laughably short, Moorish Prince took an interest in her, insisted on a hasty and arranged marriage, and immediately cast her in his controversial musical troupe. After several horrendous B movies and an affair with *General Hospital* actor, Kevin Bernhardt, Appollonia rediscovered Catholicism and fled to Rome where she took a vow of silence and experienced twice weekly bouts of stigmata. On the day of her death, it's said the rain was purple and the doves were crying. Church records negate this claim, and maintain that on the day of her funeral it was nothing more than overcast, with a couple of pigeons pecking around.

Saint Jerald, Patron Saint of Putting Up With Shit I Don't Deserve, Man

Unbeknownst to most everyone, Jesus' adoptive father, Saint Joseph (Patron Saint of Baby Aspirin) had a younger brother, Jerald, who lived in relative squalor on a houseboat in the Sea of Galilee. Though a shitty carpenter and clumsy lover, Saint Jerald was an excellent bass fisherman. One year, he even won the Jerusalem Bass Tournament, but you think anyone heard about it? No, as usual, everyone everywhere was too busy talking about Joseph-this and Joseph-that. Ooh, looky! Joseph put the Son of God through parochial school. Gasp! Sigh! Joseph married himself a virgin! Hmph. Anyway, upon Jerald's death, the Church realized they'd overlooked quite a fellow, one that had not only suffered in silence for more than 50 years, but had also built several dozen wooden decks for several dozen buddies in exchange for nothing more than a couple goatskins of wine. So, they made him a saint, but not before looting his boat and sacrificing all his sheep, which, of course, were black.

HE'S EITHER GOING TO BE REAL ATHLETIC OR A REAL JERK

The baby just drop-kicked

A head of plastic lettuce

Across the room at his preschool

Injured classmates' incident reports will read:

Hit by iceberg

IT ALSO COULD MAYBE SORTA HAVE BEEN 9/11

This country

Went downhill

When it started referring

To stuffed animals as

Plush toys

WHAT WERE THE 80s LIKE?

Men didn't wear socks

And there were more casting calls for Russians

And sometimes

At restaurants

They tossed the salad at the table instead of in the kitchen

PUT A HOLD ON MY VISA, PLEASE

That's weird. Has anyone seen my vagina? It was just here. I just had it a minute ago. I mean literally like five seconds ago. Or at least I thought I did. It's like totally disappeared. Didn't you just see me holding it? Or am I imagining things? I could've sworn I was just holding it? Odd.

Do you think I left it at the restaurant? Oh, crap. Do you think the waitress picked it up with our tab and forgot to bring it back? Do you think my vagina ended up on someone else's table? I hope not. They probably won't realize it's not theirs until they try to use it somewhere else and then someone points out that it doesn't belong to them.

I have to calm down. Think. It's got to be around here somewhere. Maybe it's in the car. Maybe I left it in the console. Or the glove compartment. Maybe I left it on the dashboard. Do you think maybe my vagina got somehow wedged between the driver's seat and the door? God. I hope not. For all I know, it could have fallen out in the middle of the interstate and been run over.

Sometimes I put it in my back pocket. I know that's a stupid thing to do, but I do it all the time when I'm in a rush. And then more often than not, it ends up in the dryer. It probably went through the wash with my jeans. Which means it won't work right if it did. It will be totally deactivated if that's the case. Shit. Then I have to wait for a replacement. That can take up to a week.

What does it look like? Is that what you're asking? To be honest, I don't really know what it looks like. I mean. Don't they all kind of look alike? Can I say that about vaginas? Don't you think they all kind of look identical? What? You don't? Really?! I'm just saying if Madison Square Garden were full of vaginas, from a distance, like on TV, they'd all pretty much look the same. Or similar. Especially if you weren't a vagina yourself. Is that racist? Really? Okay. You're telling me to shut up now.

What? Was my name on it? No. No, it wasn't. I feel like such an idiot. I can't tell you how many times I've said: You better put your name on that. Why haven't you gotten out a Sharpie and at least put your initials on that? You'll be sorry if you lose that someday and you haven't put your name on it. Dammit. I'm always doing crap like that.

Okay. I'm just going to retrace my steps. I went to the gas station. I went to the grocery. I went to the drugstore. Then I went to Starbucks and while they were making my latte, I went to the bathroom and...OH...HERE IT IS. Good grief. Here it is. Right

where you'd expect it to be. In the most obvious place all along.
Right here in my pants. Sheesh. That's a relief.

I HAVE AN IDEA FOR A DISNEY MOVIE

It's about a princess

Who says she doesn't want to be a princess

But secretly she really does want to be a princess

And by the end of the movie

You forget she ever said she didn't want to be a princess

So when she finally becomes a princess

You're really happy for her

PLEASE TELL ME SHE ALSO HAS A LIMP

Just when I thought the day couldn't get any better

The Victoria's Secret catalog arrives

With a cross-eyed cover model

HOUR ONE OF A 14-HOUR ROAD TRIP

Mom

Mom

Mom

Mommy

Mom

Mommy

Mom

Look

Look back here

Mom

Look

Look at me

Look

Look back here

I can hold my biscuit with my feet

THIS NEVER GETS OLD.
I MEAN. AT LEAST NOT FOR ME.

I love Top Gun. I love gays. I love rewriting this script the way it plays in my head.

Charlie: Excuse me, Lieutenant. Is there something wrong?

Maverick: Yes ma'am. The data on the MiG is inaccurate.

Charlie: How's that, Lieutenant?

Maverick: Well, I just happened to see a MiG 28 do a...

Goose: WE!

Maverick: Oh. Sorry, Goose. WE happened to see a MiG 28 do a 4G negative dive.

Charlie: And where did you see this?

Goose: In his pants.

Maverick: Well, technically jeans. H&M lavender matchstick jeans with this fantastic leopard detail on the ass pockets.

Goose: Leopard? I thought it was cheetah.

Maverick: Bitch, please.

Viper: Yeah, your old man did it right...We were in the worst dogfight I could've dreamed of. There were bogeys like fireflies all over the sky. His F-4 was hit. He was wounded, but he could've made it back. He stayed in it. Saved three planes before he bought it.

Maverick (daintily clapping): Oooooh!! Fireflies!

Maverick (as Charlie screeches to a halt after chasing Maverick on his motorcycle): JESUS CHRIST! AND YOU THINK I'M RECKLESS? WHEN I FLY, I'LL HAVE YOU KNOW THAT I always pack a couple of cucumber slices for puffiness.

Charlie: Well, I am going to FINISH MY SENTENCE, LIEUTENANT! My review of your flight performance...wait...what?

Maverick: And Evian. Lots of Evian.

Viper: Good morning, gentlemen, the temperature is 110 degrees.

Goose: Viper's up here! Great. Oh, shit.

Maverick: Great. He's probably saying: "Holy shit, it's Maverick and Goose. They owe me that recipe for pomegranate martinis."

Goose: Pfft. Hosehound.

Stinger: They gave you your choice of duty, son. Anything, anywhere. Do you believe that shit? Where do you think you wanna go?

Maverick: I thought of being an instructor, sir.

Stinger: Top Gun?

Maverick: No. Tap Gun.

Stinger: Tap Gun?

Maverick: It's a dance academy.

Maverick: Too close for missles, I'm switching to Kenneth Cole Reaction.

Slider: Goose, whose butt did you kiss to get in here anyway?

Goose: The list is long, but distinguished.

Slider: Yeah, well, so is my johnson.

Maverick (under his breath): God, you're so hot. I could eat you ALIVE.

Slider: What'd you say?

Maverick: Huh? Oh. I said: "How adorable. You're named after a tiny hamburger."

Iceman: You can be my wingman any time.

Maverick: Bullshit! You can be mine. I mean, as long as you don't get super-fat or something.

Maverick: So, you think I should quit?

Viper: I didn't say that. The simple fact is you feel responsible for Goose, and you have a confidence problem. Now, I'm not gonna sit here and blow sunshine up your ass, Lieutenant. A good pilot is...

Maverick: Blow sunshine up my ass?

Viper: That's right. I'm not gonna...

Maverick: Blow. Sunshine. Up. My. Ass?

Viper: Kiss your ass, Maverick. I'm not gonna...

Maverick: Kiss my ass?

Viper: Blow sunshine up your ass. Kiss your ass. They're one and the same.

Maverick: They are? Really? Because they sound different.

Viper: I'm sorry. What the fuck is going on here?

Maverick (removing aviators): I don't know, Vipey. You tell me.

I SAW SOME ARGYLE BONGS AT J.CREW

I just remembered
That Jerry Garcia
Had a line of neckties

Which begs the obvious question:

When is JoS. A. Bank
Coming out with their spring collection of one-hitters?

UNSPOKEN FACT

The child who gets up in the night the least

Is the one who is loved the most

JUST GO ON AND GIVE UP
AND START SHOPPING AT CHICO'S

Last night
I saw a bunch of stylish
Young
College girls
In skimpy sundresses
Who all had feathers in their hair
And tattoos between their shoulder blades
And I thought I might like
To try out that look for myself

Then I realized
I was only setting myself up for:
"Ma'am? That chicken on your head
Appears to have crapped
Down the back of your nightgown."

ETHAN HAWKE WILL BE MINE. ALL MINE.

There are three reasons kids go to boarding school. One, they are contrary, mule-headed children that steal their parents' champagne and molest the family dog. Two, they are gifted minorities who are sought out by administrative heads and shipped in from Malaysia, Harlem, and Omaha to diversify a campus. Three, they have just undergone some sort of domestic misfortune, usually a death or divorce, and the family thinks it best that the child start a new chapter -- in a place with lots of tweed.

Such was the case when I left Kentucky for Connecticut at 15. My brother had died in a car accident 18 months prior, and it was thought that if I were put on an automobile-free campus in a remote corner of the Berkshires, I would be exempted from this same fate.

It didn't take much convincing for me to go. Things weren't particularly sing-song at home. Plus, I'd seen *Dead Poets Society*. So, I was pretty excited to stand on a desk and scream at Robin Williams, and run through misty meadows in a woolen tracksuit, and lose my virginity to Ethan Hawke on a bed of gingko leaves. Never mind that I had the twang of Dolly Parton, the figure of Punky Brewster, was still finishing up the *Little House* books, and snorted when I laughed. Surely I could handle what awaited me

156

(How do you spell out the big-red-X-survey-says-NO sound from *Family Feud?* However it is spelled, you can insert that right here.)

Because here's what happens at boarding school, no matter how refined and elite and accelerated it may be: *Lord of the Flies.*

Let me set the scene:

On 800 deeply wooded acres, you've got 600 precocious children between the ages of 14 and 18 who are eager to smoke and poke most anything. They are lorded over by 150 borderline alcoholic teachers with Ivy League degrees who have somehow agreed to live in dormitories with teenagers who don't feel like reading Chaucer but do feel like urinating in a trashcan and throwing it out a sixth-story window. There's lots of Pink Floyd, marijuana being shipped in in coffee cans, and vodka in Prell bottles. Add to that, two hours of daily sports and five hours of daily homework and the kids I described above (rebellious rich kids, brilliant poor kids, kids who don't speak English, kids who've been airlifted off a pig farm, kids who've had to choose between living with mom or living with dad, and kids who've just gone to a funeral).

It was a divine disaster, I tell you. Divine. The freedom you could attain if you could learn how to effectively dodge authority was glorious. And the girls' dorm I lived in was the worst. While the boys were across campus, rolling their own cigarettes, playing nickel poker, and participating in jolly pranks involving talcum powder and cans of trick peanuts, the gals where I resided were kicking through drywall, turning over soda machines, and spraying Lysol on the bathrooms walls then setting it on fire. Have you ever seen the word PENIS glowing on a dark lavatory wall, while some faculty member four floors down just pours himself another whiskey? Liberating. Thank goodness the school was co-ed. Those fellows tempered us. Several miles away at an all-girls school, I heard they were just having sex with cows and swallowing knives.

Moving right along, one of our rituals involved a bicycle. There was a sorry, old ten-speed chained to the basement handrail in our dorm, and from five stories up, you could peer straight down through the metal bannister and see that dusty bike seat 40-something feet below, just begging for a goober. We didn't know who the bike belonged to, but we were pretty sure it was a teacher. So, with every trip down those stairs, there was some target practice going on.

Everyone partook.

Hey, Joan. Where you headed?
Oh, down to paddle tennis.
Cool. I'm heading to the snack bar to buy a dozen chocolate chip cookies that I'm going to emotional power-eat with my hands

tied behind my back. Hey! Let's spit on the bike seat!

Oh, yes! Let's!

Hi there, Angela! What's shakin'?

My tits.

Rad. Want to go see what movie the A/V Club is showing? It might be *Deliverance* or *The Wall* or *The Godfather.*

Oh, no thanks. I'm just heading down to the Language Lab to study German for that teacher who rips off my miniskirt with his eyes. Want to spit on the bike seat with me on the way out?

Twist my rubber arm.

Howdy, Polly. Where to?

Fuckin' math.

Fuck that shit.

Damn right.

(spit)

(spit)

So, the point here is that there are lots of fun things to do at boarding school besides writing essays on bird symbolism in *Invisible Man* and conjugating the French future perfect. Why, you can throw a pack of 500 firecrackers out the window during study hall and have the school shut down for "rapid gunfire alert." You can play soccer in a freak October snow until your feet are bleeding and nobody gives a shit. (And when I say nobody, I mean NOBODY!) Or you can spit on a bike seat so many times that you really could go to the Olympics for spitting. Because everyone knows that rituals as such, will bring you good luck. It is one small thing you can master in a place where little is masterable. You will probably not go to Yale. You will probably not make the Headmaster's List. You will probably not make it across the lunchroom, from your table in the corner to where you will dump your tray, without being accosted about the rise of your pants or the fall of your skirt, but you can eventually hit that seat 97% of the time and that will make Ethan Hawke fall in love with you.

(Originally appeared in a similar form on Loop)

JUST SHOOT ME

Here's something I never thought I'd say:

"What's your daily rate for hamster boarding?"

THAT'S A CUTE LABOR DAY OUTFIT

Temperature-wise

It's that awkward "between seasons" time of year

When I inevitably

Have to wear pantyhose

Under my bathing suit

For a couple of weeks

MY OPEN MIC GOAL

To make crowds of 16

Slightly less depressed

One fallopian tube joke at a time

BURYING BEETLE MOTHER

So, kids. I don't know if you've been paying any attention whatsoever to *The Today Show*, but it just so turns out I'm not the worst mother in the world. I know!! Shocker, huh?! Yeah. So, the worst mother out there is actually what they call a Tiger Mother.

The Tiger Mother makes her kids practice the violin for like four hours a day. The Tiger Mother refuses to buy a television. And all the Tiger Mother ever allows her kids for snacks are raw, unsalted Brussels sprouts served with a spork. What? How does a baby tiger play the violin? Like everyone else, silly! With a bow! Geez Louise. Are you paying attention?

So, you ask. If I'm not a Tiger Mother, what kind of mother am I? Good question. I'm so glad you're interested. Apparently, after much research on the first website that popped up on my Google search, I'm most closely related to the Burying Beetle Mother.

For starters, the Burying Beetle Mother lives inside a mouse carcass, and, being resourceful, lays her eggs inside its corpse. Soon enough, the eggs hatch and the larvae move into the rodent's rotting flesh. The Burying Beetle Mother takes great care of her young larvae by eating dead mouse meat, regurgitating it, and sharing it with her babies.

Now. Who does that sound like, kids? Who can you think of who's that generous? Me??? You're right! Just like I share my Domino's with you, the Burying Beetle Mother always shares her dead mouse vomit with her offspring! Don't I always, always give you my stuffed crusts? Yes, I do, thank you very much.

Now, true, the Burying Beetle Mother more often than not eats her own children. But she only eats the ones who annoy her. The squeaky wheels. The buggers. The kids who can't keep their pie holes shut. The ones who don't stop whining on the way back from Target about how I was so mean not to buy the Boba Fett sleeping bag that everyone else in Cub Scouts has. Those are the only ones she devours. For the most part, she's extremely loving and wise and patient. And when the larvae grow into beetles and move out of the mouse carcass, she always buys them their own, pre-owned, gently-used, scratch-and-dent iPhone.

Much better than a Tiger Mother, right?

WHEN WAS THE WAR OF 1812?

They just described
Someone on the news
As having the mental capacity
Of a 12-year-old

Um
That's good, right?
I'm just asking
Because I no longer
Know the difference
Between a radius and a diameter

SHHHHHHHHH

Hush now

Don't tell David Spade

That I'm wearing his tits

LOOK! I MADE A DAISY CHAIN!

Scientists have discovered

Some new particle

That explains

Why matter has mass

I don't even know what that means

Thank goodness for people like this

Because if people like me

Were in charge of the world

We'd be sleeping under piles of leaves

And making up annoying jingles

SEXUAL POSITIONS OF
OLD, TIRED MARRIED COUPLES

The Folded Lawn Chair

This occurs when the wife, mistakenly thinking she still weighs on the low end of 120, straddles her husband in his Tempur-Pedic lawn chair. A spilled Sanka, a ripped pair of Spanx, and two cracked skulls later, no one is any closer to climax.

Hot Carlos

When the lawn boy's a dead ringer for Javier Bardem, every Wednesday the wife will be in the mood for a little role play. Begin by getting a spray tan and brushing up on your Canary Island Spanish, then set the mood by spreading lime with your large, calloused hands and drinking in slow-motion from the garden hose. Don't forget to wear some cutoffs, a sleeveless flannel, and a pair of loosely laced work boots! Oh. And most importantly? A bag on your head.

Go Lie Down, Doggy

Missionary style, wearing Six Flags sweatshirts, while the family dog looks on in pity. Or is it disgust?

Fiery Saddle

In this instance, position doesn't matter, just somebody slips a disc.

Catholic Saddle

The same as above except somebody's screaming:

JESUSMARYANDJOSEPHMYGODFORSAKENBACK!!!!!!

Cleveland Arcade

While the husband watches online porn, the wife repeatedly asks: "Do these Kohl's capris make my ass look fat?"

Oral Roberts

That one time a year, after a viewing of *Pretty Woman*, that the wife does that thing. You know, the thing that requires you to buy something from Tiffany's.

I AM Your Daddy

Foreplay on a playroom couch that leads to an unintentional lightsaber probing.

Hide The Toblerone

No, seriously. Hide it. Your husband desperately wants to devour your candy bar. And sadly, candy bar isn't code for anything.

The Jimmy Fallon

I don't care what we do, just so long as I can still see the television.

Dusty Heather

After coming across your high school yearbook in the attic, you'll come across your high school yearbook in the attic.

Lazy Pirate

When the bedroom door won't lock, somebody's gotta keep one eye open for the kids. (A variation on this theme involves one spouse passing out on Captain Morgan's.)

Arizona Hot Pocket

Your relatives in Phoenix always put us on the pull-out couch, right in the middle of the living room. But that's not going to stop me from trying.

J.R. Ewing

Tell you what. Why don't I "work late" while you drink yourself into an asylum.

Alaskan Pipeline

Between the kids' bedtime and *Deadliest Catch*, maybe we could...What? We missed last week's episode and it's on right now? Well, never mind! I'll be taking a raincheck on what was certain to be a half-hearted jack anyway, thankyouverymuch.

Oily Bow Tie

After a flat tire in the pouring rain -- while the wife and kids look on and the AAA guy is way late -- the husband pretends to strangle himself while yelling "Oh, FUCK me!"

(Originally appeared in a similar form on HowAboutWe)

APRIL 2ND

Just a reminder
That today is
April Idiot's Day

In honor of those
Who keep falling for yesterday's pranks

IT'S TRUE

Every time Gwyneth sings country music

An angel rips its wings off

And every time Natalie Portman gives an acceptance speech

A ballerina explodes

DO YOU THINK IT'S WEED OR ALCOHOL?

Hank

Has been passed out all day

In the top of his hamster rotunda

In a pool of his own urine

Proving once again

We should have made him get a job this summer

Instead of one more year of swim team

FRENCH SAMMY HAGAR NEEDS YOUR MONEY

I get a lot of spam emails. This one is French. I took French for 10 years. My translation appears in italics.

Bonjour! Contribuent au transfert de manquer Aliyaah et Samar moghter.

Good morning/daytime-ish! Contribute to the mannequin transfer of Aaliyah and Sammy Hagar's mother.

J'ai 20 ans avec mon jeune frère qui a 17 ans. Nous avons perdu nous parents, et nous avons un héritage de nos parents en retard.

I am 20 years old with my young brother who is 17 years old. We lost our parents at Purdue, and we have a heritage of mentally challenged parents.

Nos parents étaient des agriculteurs très riches sur le cacao et le marchand de bananes quand ils étaient vivants.

Our parents had agricultural riches on the hot chocolate (cocaine?) and marched with bananas in a parade that was vivacious.

Après la mort de mon père, il ya longtemps, ma mère a été le contrôle de son activité économique jusqu'à ce qu'elle a été empoisonné par ses associés d'affaires dont elle a souffert et est mort.

After the death of my father, for a long time, my mother was a control freak with her son's economic class just because she was poisoned in the summer for having an affair with an associate who died from eating a souffle.

Avant la mort de notre mère en mai 2009 dans un hôpital privé ici en Angleterre Royaume-Uni où elle a été admise, elle m'a secrètement appelé sur son chevet et m'a révélé qu'elle a la somme de dollars américains quatorze millions sept cent (14,7 millions de dollars) qu'elle a quitté en compte d'attente dans l'une des banque ici en Angleterre Royaume-KIGDOM, no one is even going to notice if I write the word cocksucker in the middle of this maybe not even the word shitbaby maybe not even turd burglar Joan of Arc was most definitely bisexual Napoleon couldn't even find his own penis I have a great recipe for kale chips que c'était l'argent qu'elle avait l'intention de transférer à l'investissement avant sa mort soudaine, elle m'a également informé que je devrais chercher un associé étranger dans n'importe quel pays de mon choix qui aidera me transférer cet argent en compte bien où l'argent sera enregistrer et judicieusement investis.

Sweet Jesus, the amount of accent marks is excessive. The mother died in 2009 in a private hospital.

En raison du taux élevé des taxes de l'investissement en Angleterre qui est pourquoi j'ai décidé de vous contacter afin de nous aider transférer l'argent dans votre pays où il sera mettre de l'investissement. J'aimerai que vous m'aidiez dans ces domaines: *Raisins, England, taxes, and the like:*

1. Pour fournir un compte bancaire sûr, où l'argent sera transféré dans l'investissement. Et pour nous aider à trouver un très bonne affaire lucreative dans votre pays où nous pouvons investir de l'argent.

2. Pour servir de gardien de ces fonds puisque j'ai seulement 20 ans et mon frère est encore trop jeunes pour gérer ce type de transaction.

3. Pour prendre des dispositions pour moi et mon btother de venir à votre pays pour notre éducation et de garantir un titre de séjour pour nous dans votre pays.

1. High shimmy

2. Low shimmy

3. Everywhere you go shimmy

Moi et mon frère ont décidé de vous offrir 15% du montant total de votre volonté de nous aider, S'il vous plaît veuillez réponse à mon mail immédiatement à vos informations personnelles, numéro de téléphone afin que nous puissions discuter avec vous au téléphone.

Act now and receive 15% off Cindy Crawford's Meaningful Beauty. The French are attacking. Here's a phone number. Just kidding, the French don't attack people, they just demean them. Goldfish. But I did steal your identity.

Merci et soyez bénis,

Votre Aliyaah et Samar moghter

Thank you and soybeans,

Your Aaliyah and Sammy Hagar's mother

POWER OUTAGE

What have I learned
From 27 hours without the Internet?

That every once in a while
It's really important
To get back to human interaction

And have a face-to-face conversation
About how you don't have
Internet access

GOING ONCE, GOING TWICE

I've got a certified, pre-owned breast pump (2006)

That I'm looking to trade

For a new

Unboxed

iPad 3

Next up:

A half bag of cat food

For a week in Vail

It's Friskies Mixed Seafood Blend

We prefer ski-in/ski-out

IT ONLY COST 99 CENTS AT OLD NAVY

The whoopie cushion

We bought today

Has become a source of

Hyperventilating laughter

And all family members are rushing to name each output

Winners so far

"Broccoli Casserole"

"Duck, Duck, Screech"

"The Party Favor"

"Burnt Coffee"

and

"Hello, Guadalajara"

A long, high-pitched wail

Can only be achieved by masters of the cushion

This is known as

"Mariah's Kidney Stone"

WHAT KIND OF A SICKO ARE YOU?

A lot of women complain that men are horrible at being sick. That at the first sign of a sniffle, the male persuasion is quick to whine and wail, plant their feverish bodies front-and-center on a couch they've moved into an entrance hall, surround themselves with Himalayas of Kleenex, and hire out someone to plaster the nearest billboard with: "JOE HAS A REALLY BAD SINUS INFECTION." Some of these men, I've heard, even employ a little silver bell. That they ring when they need something. Like orange juice. Or Robitussin. Or someone who actually gives a flying fuck that they're congested.

I have to give my husband credit. When he's sick, no one really knows it. Maybe it's because I banish him to the basement sectional and throw Powerade down the stairs to him every eighteen hours. Or maybe it's because he's usually the fourth and last to get whatever's been going through our house, and I've already been rendered deaf from whining. But for the most part, he's a silent sufferer.

Not me. I like everyone to know damn well that I've been infected by no fault of my own. I wash my hands. I do not pick my nose. I do not suck my thumb. I certainly do not go into jumpy castles and lick the inflatable floor. I do not chew gum that I've discovered on the sole of my shoe. Nor do I go to the gym and lift other people's sweaty weights before drinking out of a public water fountain. NO! I proudly live in a self-created halo of hand sanitizer, however, about twice a year, one of my sons decides to vomit into my eyeball, thus shattering my antibacterial bubble and rendering me gravely ill.

Here's the shitty thing about being sick as a mom: you still have the same schedule to keep. All that crap you were doing in a sweater set and pearls (or in my case, a microfleece union suit and rainboots) is the same crap you've got to keep doing with blood coming out of your ears. So, I don't like getting sick. And when I do, I make a point of keeping everyone on Facebook updated about my antibiotics regime and its associated side effects. (On a side note: I do suffer the big things in domestic silence. I don't mention the pain of childbirth, the pain of breastfeeding, or the pain of episiotomies. I spare my husband and sons the details of such things and save that material for the local open mic.) Thus, in this household at least, it's the girl who is bad at being sick. But I do smell good. That is, if you like Lysol.

So, what sort of sick person are you? (Or should I say "What sort of ILL person are you?" lest you think I'm talking about pedophiles.) Here are some popular suffering styles. Can you find you or your mate?

The Vocalist

As previously described, this patient doesn't suffer quietly. He or she sneezes into microphones, sniffles into megaphones, and violently wheezes throughout the house, just to drive home the point that: YES. I have come down with SOMETHING. Maybe even SMALLPOX. This tickle in my throat? It's not a cough. It's a raccoon that needs hacking up during your important business call/nap/championship game. But don't worry about me. I'll get your LAUNDRY DONE.

The Invalid

This is a bedridden Vocalist who adores pity. Rendered completely immobile by something as simple as hayfever, this convalescent will take to the sheets at the first sign of a splinter. Get your butler bells, baby talk, and bedpans ready for this beauty. They're going nowhere. And they need you, RIGHT NOW, to feed them some Earl Grey out of an eyedropper while you sing "You Are My Sunshine."

Dead Man (or Woman) Walking

Much like my husband, this martyr refuses to succumb to illness and insists on staggering along as if nothing is happening. An attack of leprosy? No problem. Let me just put my forearm into my briefcase and keep going. You can easily identify this species, as they often show up for important meetings with eyes swollen shut, smelling of Vicks VapoRub, and using sign language.

Frequently, they just die on the subway on their way to buy some Tic Tacs for tuberculosis.

The Sicko

The variety insists on describing, in great detail, the fouler parts of his or her affliction, such as: warts, cysts, seepage and excretions, things related to the digestive and reproductive tracts, gangrene, trenchfoot, flesh-eating diseases, all manner of discharge, and snot. Would you like to see their scar? No? Here it is anyway.

The Cold Case

These individuals always have some sort of vague, undiagnosed ailment -- usually accompanied by a cold or malaise or exhaustion. Unlike the loud vocalist, this character likes to mope. And sigh. And pout. The best thing you can do for these folks is to suggest they open a Twitter account (the modern version of: "Here's a quarter, call someone who cares."). I'm not saying these chronically ill people have a psychological problem that makes them want constant attention, but actually I am.

Darwin's Dream

Every once in a while, you come across a species of humanoid that never, ever gets sick. These people bounce through life, loaded with both vim and vitamin C. They're always going somewhere or getting back from somewhere, like floating down the Amazon on flu victims or descending Everest with those who "couldn't deal" strapped to their backs. They like to say: "I never get sick!!! Sickness is something you CHOOSE!" These people don't usually die from disease, instead they're poisoned by the people they live with.

(Originally appeared in a similar form on HowAboutWe)

HEAT INDEX 115

I was going to give the kids an egg

To fry on the driveway

But we're out of eggs

So I gave them a hot dog

But then the cat ate it

WOULD YOU LIKE A BITE?

Mom? What are you eating?

A blood orange

WHAT?!?!?!?!?!?!?!?!?!?!?!!!!!!!!!

You heard me

JUST A HUNCH

I drove past campus earlier today

And saw this big group of girls

Just hanging out on a curb

Sprawled in various ways on top of a big pile of

Pink and purple and zebra stripe and leopard print hard-shell

luggage

There was a broken-down bus next to them

And all the girls had their lace tank tops

Tucked into their bras

And were wearing shorts that I think were actually

Handkerchiefs tucked into their buttocks

And they all had the same, blank, dumbfounded look on their

faces

Just staring off into space

Chewing gum like a bunch of cattle

That had just been asked to convert miles into kilometers

And all I could think was:

That is probably not a Women's Studies bus

MOVIES BASED ON TRUE STORIES

The Runway's End

A traveling salesman gets snowed in at the Kansas City airport.
He does not meet his soul mate at the Terminal D bar. He does
not overcome years of crippling self-hatred by loudly berating the
ticket agent. And he does not encounter a gay politician in the
men's room. He does, however, end up staying at the airport's
Courtyard by Marriott, where he eats an old bagel for dinner
and watches the last half of *Law & Order* before finding a pubic
hair in the ice bucket. The next morning, he wakes up with a
crick in his neck, then flies back to his flat-chested wife in
Greensboro.

Ollie and Friskers

Ollie the French bulldog and Friskers the tabby cat get accidently
left behind when their owners move. The pets begin a long
journey home by navigating forests, torrential downpours, and
junkyards. Friskers loses a leg to a coyote. Ollie gets Lyme
disease. And even though they end up dying slowly and sadly
from exposure, when people see them trotting along in the
interstate's median, they do imagine Friskers being voiced by
Dakota Fanning and Ollie by Tim Allen.

Here Come the Zombies

At 5:05 a.m. on a Sunday, after lots of red wine the night before, a disheveled mother makes waffles for her toddler, while her husband eats a handful of Rolaids before passing out, face down, in the newspaper's sports section.

My Crazy Bridesmaid

A nutjob bridesmaid ruins a wedding by making a pass at the groom and wearing shoes that are decidedly fuchsia and NOT salmon. It would be nice if a heartfelt toast made up for everything in the end, or if a dazzling wedding gift was given as a peace offering. But the whole time she's on her honeymoon, the bride just ends up yammering on and on about how much she totally hates the bridesmaid, forcing the groom to pretty much drink his way through St. Croix and wonder what the hell he's just done with the rest of his life.

Greasy Days

This documentary follows several dozen people and their fast food eating habits over the course of a few months. None of them gets heart disease or food poisoning, and most of them don't eat out all that often, but when they do, 51% prefer chicken to beef even if the chicken is fried because it just sort of seems healthier. Also, a few people sometimes eat in their cars so they can listen to *The Clark Howard Show*.

My Reliable Love

At a 25th high school reunion, a divorced woman marches

straight past her sophomore year boyfriend, straight past the nerd who ended up cute, and straight past the former quarterback, and directly to the veggie tray where she sees, with much delight, that the ranch dip is Hidden Valley brand.

Into the Danger Zone
A young man goes off to war and his girlfriend pines for him daily. That is, until she starts working at the Tat Shack and falls for a guy named Rico. The soldier doesn't have any battle scenes, but he does take up dipping Skoal. After about 6 months, he realizes that his love-hate relationship with the desert is actually more hate.

Something's Going On
In a regular suburban house -- a house that looks just like any other -- a family is besieged by terror when they start hearing strange sounds and misplacing small valuables. Then they find out their iguana has a cold and that the Molly Maids are common thieves.

Search for the Milky Way
A kid dressed as an astronaut raids his sister's Halloween candy.

Wall Street III
A banker gets laid off but it's okay because he really likes

cupcakes and is pretty decent at baking and there's kind of a cupcake craze going on these days anyway.

One of God's Children

Deep in the slums of Bombay, there's a boy who knows nothing about game show trivia. But he will provide sexual favors for a teaspoon of couscous.

(Originally appeared in a similar form on The Big Jewel)

I BUY THE $7 BOX OF HAIR BLEACH THAT HAS A PICTURE OF GWEN STEFANI ON THE FRONT NEXT TO AN ASTERISK AND THEN A PICTURE OF GUNNAR NELSON ON THE BACK NEXT TO AN ASTERISK

Guesses of my natural haircolor:

Kettle Corn

Burnt Sienna

Stump

Metallic Blah

Crouton

Earl Grey Grey

Snapple Backwash

Lady-Who-Has-Less-Fun Brownishness

Chicken Finger

Glaucoma

Platypus

Hobo's Tongue

(Let's call it a day with Denture Stain)

YODA'S PEARLS OF WISDOM FOR NEW PARENTS

The force, yes. It everywhere is. Even in that diaper. Huge it is.

The baby to sleep put. Then vodka you can drink.

Spank do not. Unless you want your child a drug addict to be.

Sex never again you will have. Unless for it you pay.

His mind Yoda change. That baby a Sith be. Spank you must.

The dark side I sense in you. To formula I think you should switch.

Twilight is upon me. Soon night must fall. For you? Not so much.

Vaginal birth more painful than c-section is. There. Yoda that argument solve.

Wookiees great nannies make.

LADIES ALSO LIKE TO PAY THEIR OWN WAY AT THE GOLDEN CORRAL

That Cialis ad that ends with
A man and a woman
In his-and-hers bathtubs at
The carnival

Uh
Call me high-maintenance
But that might be the
WORST DATE EVER

If you're gonna splurge
And take me to the state fair for a public bath
I guess you expect
Four hours of sex afterward?

I wonder
When they were coming up with that commercial
In the conference room
How did that conversation
Among ad executives go?

"What do women like, Bill?"
"Oh. That's easy. Ferris wheels and unrelenting erections."

JOINT DUH STUDIES

Studies suggest that exercising on uneven pavement can injure your knees. As will banging on them with a hammer, an iron frying pan, or any other heavy object. "It's amazing the damage one jog on a pothole-covered road can do to the average man," says orthopedic surgeon Dr. Jon Galveston. "Remarkably, the same holds true for beating on your kneecaps with a manhole cover."

Just 30 minutes of brisk walking in spandex can reduce your cancer risk by 19% but simultaneously increase your risk of being wet Willie-ed and having your buttocks duct-taped together by 23.6%.

Turns out, most people hate liver. And Katie Couric.

You can drastically reduce your number of friends and acquaintances by an astounding 74% by simply giving them your 55-minute acai berry juice presentation. Or showing them your testicles. Statistically, pyramid schemes and balls are equally offensive.

89% of Finns think their flag is boring, while 40% of Chinese prefer the Chinese yo-yo to a yo-yo made in China.

A joint study out of England shows that unmarried men are more likely than married men to develop heart disease, and, overall, Americans are happy as shit they didn't humiliate their sausages by naming them "bangers."

A recent study showed that drinking orange juice can provide health benefits, most notably a boost in an individual's vitamin C levels. Also, Ashton Kutcher is sorry he ever married Demi Moore. Contrary to popular belief, vitamin C does not reduce the severity of the common cold, nor does Demi Moore look good once you're within three feet of her face. However, vitamin C can protect the body against oxidative stress and Ashton takes some solace in the fact he can still pull off the trucker hat.

A 2010 travel study showed that 85% of airline passengers prefer both the aisle seat and their pretzels rat turd-free.

42% of Americans approve of the President. 38% of Americans think Helen Hunt is a man. And 20% of Americans think Laura Linney is Helen Hunt.

It's been proven that babies who are breastfed may have IQs two to three points higher than their bottle-fed peers. In addition, most local car dealerships have poorly written jingles that, despite their suckiness, STILL get stuck in your head. Screw you,

Enfamil. And screw you, Bobby Beaverton's Chevy-Buick-Pontiac.

WHO DO YOU THINK WE ARE? THE OSMONDS?

The Collins boys
Just performed their first song
On two toy guitars

I think it was titled:

"STOP. Please Stop That Incessant Twanging. Property Values
Are Plummeting And Small Animals Are Exploding."

STEVE JOBS'S OBITUARY

Other than iCarly

A spotless career

I HOPE IT WASN'T HAM AND PINEAPPLE

OMG

I just ran over a pizza box

on New Circle Road

I don't even know where it came from

It was just all of a sudden there

In front of me

I didn't even have time to swerve

Or brake

I feel sick inside

I can't get the sound out of my head

YOU'RE DOING IT ALL WRONG!

If you're married or living together, it's probably already apparent who excels at which chores. In this household, I only had to hang a few pictures using my clog to hammer a lugnut into the wall before my husband took over that task. And my husband only had to decorate one shelf with an old biology textbook and a peeling Rubik's Cube before I became the accessorizer. When it comes to claiming a domestic duty, the key is not so much discovering what you're good at, but discovering what you CAN'T STAND watching someone else do.

For example...

The Dishwasher
Watching my husband load the dishwasher is a retina-burning cataclysm that no human should witness. In fact, a video of him loading tumblers sideways in the top rack is the only movie they feature on Hell Airways besides *From Justin to Kelly* and old-people porn. There's unrinsed, oily Tupperware; pans nesting inside pans like Russian dolls; and butcher knives crammed inside baby bottles. Five plates stuck together with refried beans? Load them as a single unit topped with a collander. Out of dishwashing gel? Squeeze in a bottle of Log Cabin. Because surely after a 20-minute cycle of tepid water, all this shit will come out looking like the holy grail. How could it not? We spent a whopping $250 on a

dishwasher made by Frigidaire. Never mind that Mr. Frigidaire got his start making appliances to keep ICE CREAM FROM MELTING, I'm sure this modern miracle can handle a saucepan of bacon grease and a couple of Halloween wigs that need sterilizing.

Anyway, I'm getting carried away, but long story short: my husband is not allowed near the dishwasher. EVER. (Except to empty it like twice a day.)

Packing the Car

You'd think with my mad dishwasher skills I'd be able to load a minivan, but when I pack for two kids and myself, the wheels quickly fall off the wagon. What starts as a noble intention to have all things relegated to separate Ziplocs and totes, soon devolves into the sort of yard sale insane people have. Halfway through, I start treating the car like a plate of nachos. I throw videos and diapers and blankets and sticker books and bottles of Tylenol and phone chargers and *People* magazines into the minivan like it's doused in kerosene and set to explode. Then after I press the children inside, padded by snorkels, I top everything off with a couple of handfuls of pretzels and string cheese. Because a sprinkling of food that is now between the seats will certainly tide them over until we get to Miami.

But back to my point: only my husband can do this packing-of-the-vehicle thing. And he does it pretty awesomely. I know they'd invite him to be a Navy Seal if he just showed them our trunk. I mean, that's how you get to be a Navy Seal, right?

Making the Bed

I couldn't make a bed any better had I been raised and beaten by a British schoolmarm. Every week, I wash the sheets in bleach and scalding water as if they'd last been used by a maternity ward. Next, I tuck everything in, blankets included, using hospital corners. See that bedspread? It's tighter than Joan Rivers's face. And the throw pillows? Well, they have designated spots. It's like a well-choreographed episode of *Glee*.
Were this bed-making task left to my husband? We'd sleep on a mattress covered in beach towels and remote controls.

The Grocery Shopping

Oh, I'm good at this. Really good. The problem is, I shop like I'm some sort of goddamned celebrity. My husband will give me the weekly grocery budget, and I'll return 10 minutes later with two, Frisbee-sized filet mignons, one roll of Viva (do you hear the angels singing?) paper towels, and a couple of lawn chairs. You think they don't sell patio furniture at the grocery store? I'll prove you wrong by turning my yard into a living room.

Anyway, I can't budget this sort of crap called "feeding the family." My husband is excellent at this. He'll take the same amount of money, clip a bunch of coupons, and return with cereals and milk and beans and vegetables. He'll also probably have 15 to 20 pounds of "manager's special" tilapia that is loaded with contaminants, but with all these chores, I'm willing to consume something that might cause me to grow an extra hand or two. Or maybe even a tail.

So, dear lovers. Take it from me. Make one of those totally sexy job charts for you and your mate. It's excellent for your relationship. You may think I'm kidding, but nothing's a bigger turn-on than never having to watch someone misuse a dustpan.

(Originally appeared in a similar form on HowAboutWe)

SEPTEMBER

Everyone is always

So sad

When the pool closes

But I'm just happy

To quit getting

Fecal contamination emails

SAVE ME A CORNER PIECE

Baby is to crib as cake is to oven

Do not turn on light

Do not open the door

Do not mess with the thermostat

Do not poke

Do not check

Do not touch

When the baby is done sleeping

You will know by scent

Also

An inserted toothpick will come out clean

Let cool before icing

I ALSO LOVE PICKLED BEETS

Are you growing and canning
Your own food?
I hope so
Because when Armageddon comes
I'll need people to steal from

Just so you know
I like corn relish
Stewed tomatoes
Bread-and-butter cucumbers
Cured ham (preferably Virginian)
And runner beans

You can keep the sauerkraut

It's also a personal touch
When the Mason jar lid is covered in gingham
And tied with twine

But don't put yourself out

FACEBOOK FRIEND #316
IS JUST ASKING FOR RAT POISON

Status Update: Is it just me, or does the Starbucks on North Elm totally smell like smoked ham?

Comment 1: Exactly!!

Comment 2: More like cod, IMHO!

Comment 3: LMFAO. Smoked ham!

Friend #316: Dude. Did I leave my Steelers hat over there after the Superbowl?

Status Update: Worst. Traffic. Ever.

Comment 1: I-95?

Comment 2: Same here. Construction.

Friend #316: Sorry to hear about you and Karen, man.

Status Update: Geez! This weather! One more snowflake and I'm going postal!

Comment 1: I'm moving to Florida.

Comment 2: Sunshine please!!!!!

Comment 3: So over snow.

Friend #316: How'd the colonoscopy go?

Status Update: AWESOME GAME! Barn burner.

Friend #316: How's your sister doing? She still having trouble?

Status Update: Mmmmm! Tacos!!

Friend #316: You ever get that thing looked at?

Status Update: Crazy. Had one of those damn falling dreams last night.

Comment 1: Better than one of those dreams where you can't run!

Comment 2: Probably means you're stressed out.

Friend #316: Holy crap. I haven't had one of those since 10th grade. Remember 10th? What was that hot girl's name again? The one you said you'd kill your own mother just to titty fuck? LOL!! WHAT was her name?!?!?!

Status Update: Anybody have a good teriyaki marinade recipe?

Comment 1: I just use soy sauce and honey.

Comment 2: Have you checked Emeril?

Friend #316: Kathy James! That was her name, man!!! The 10th grader! Holy shit! Her name was Kathy James!

Comment 4: Try Kikkoman.

Kathy James: Nice.

OH. MY. HOW THOUGHTFUL.

When you live with boys
You never know what
You're going to come across

But a half-eaten breakfast sausage link
Wrapped in a paper towel
And left on the back of the toilet
Has really upped the ante

GEOGRAPHICAL LOVE LIMERICKS

Probably Should Have Stuck With Tennis

There once was a man from Toledo,

Who took icy swims in his Speedo.

The shrinkage was so bad,

It damaged his gonads

And totally killed his libido.

Rock the Cradle of Love

Ethel, my girlfriend's, from Boulder.

She's what you might call a bit older.

And after our nookie,

She serves milk and cookies,

Then gives me a burp on her shoulder.

Get the ASPCA on His Ass

My boyfriend from Concord, New Hampshire,

Was sexy and hot, that's for damn sure.

But he liked it quite kinky

And ran off with Pinky --

My poor little hairless pet hamster.

Idaho, You Da Ho

I dated a woman from Boise --

Obnoxious and bossy and noisy.

Orange was her skin.

Her height? Four-foot-ten.

I drugged her and shipped her to Jersey.

QADDAFI (GADDAFHI, KADAWFFEY, CADOFFIE) IS DEAD

YAY!

Time to reclaim the beret

Or

More realistically

Adult acne

THE ONLY THING THAT MAKES ME ANGRIER
THAN A PINK MOPED IS NUCLEAR WAR

I just got cut off in traffic

By a female college student

On a pink moped

Who was NOT wearing a helmet

But WAS wearing flip flops with big bows on them

Then she pulled into Starbucks

And parked in a handicapped spot

Looks like Fuck U. is back in session

WHEN I WAS YOUR AGE: BABYSITTER EDITION

Child: I don't like Miss Shirley. Miss Shirley doesn't play Legos.

Parent: Oh, you poor dear. When I was your age in 1978, the babysitters didn't play Legos either. No, they preferred something called "hide the salami." Ah, memories. It was actually pretty fun until the ether wore off.

Child: My favorite babysitter is Courtney. She's pretty and she smells good and she lets me play on her iPhone. Why don't we get Courtney anymore?

Parent: Have you looked at your mother lately? Do you see the atrocity that is my ass in these sweatpants? Do you smell the smell of soy milk emanating off this Member's Only jacket that I am wearing without a bra because I couldn't find any other clothes other than the ones in the Goodwill bag and I haven't done laundry in weeks? Do you know what it does to my self-esteem to have someone come in here with glutes like two cinnamon rolls and a voice like maple syrup? When I was your age, all the sitters smelled like clam chowder and suggested we ram knitting needles into our navels. And they looked like burn victims in quilted housecoats. So, to answer your question, I've had Courtney killed.

Child: Mom? I don't think Jill knows CPR.

Parent: When I was your age, CPR hadn't been invented. When

children were stupid enough to cram a wine cork down their trachea, adults didn't know what else to do but finish the wine and watch as the gene pool improved itself.

Child: You're going away for two nights? TWO WHOLE NIGHTS? And you're leaving me in my own home with my own grandmother? It's SO UNFAIR!

Parent: I can see how you'd feel that way. Because, when I was 3, my parents went to Germany for 15 days and left me with an elderly woman named Mrs. Seamond who fed me margarine for dinner and then put me to bed for the night at 3:15 in the afternoon. For two weeks, all we did was drive around the beltline in her Dodge while she drank Listerine. Sometimes, if I was lucky, she'd let me pluck her chin hairs before breakfast -- which was two prunes and a tea bag. Then, when my parents returned, they brought me a coffee table book on Auschwitz and a music box made out of pork casings. So, I can see how you'd be disappointed that you're going to eat pizza for 48 hours and be given a scooter upon our return. Let me go on and call the therapist.

Child: But what if I get sick or hurt? Does the sitter know your cell phone number?

Parent: When I was your age, cell phones didn't exist. When children became ill or injured in the days of Trans Ams, sitters were put on hold by the country club staff until the grown ups had finished their gimlets. That's why it was helpful if sitters knew a thing or two about blood tranfusions and Last Rites. Which they didn't.

Child: Where did you find this sitter? How do you know if she's going to be nice?
Parent: Because I spent five weeks researching, interviewing, calling previous employers, and spending $250 on background checks. What you're getting is a Mary Poppins in skinny jeans and flip flops who has a firm knowledge of both Beyblades and EpiPens. Why, when I was your age, sitters were collected at the women's prison bus stop and paid in lentils. Where do you think I learned how to dance? Now, go bring Mommy a box cutter. She has to remove her left lung. That's how much it costs me to have someone watch you while I go to The UPS Store.

NUTS ARE FINE, TOO

If you're a grown man
Who makes a living
Singing children's music

I hope you had to pay for that ukulele
With your amputated penis

BEACHCOMBING

A day at the shore

Isn't complete

Until somebody finds a rock

Shaped like a gun

Wait

That's not a rock

It's a hip replacement

FINISH THE FAMOUS MOVIE QUOTE

Top Gun

Maverick: What's your problem, Kazanski?

Iceman: You're everyone's problem. That's because every time you go up in the air, you're unsafe. I don't like you because you're_____.

A) dangerous

B) foolhardy

C) short as shit

D) devil-may-care

E) always saying you're going to call or drop by or that we should do something sometime, but all I ever hear is Goose this and Hollywood that and Viper this and Kenny Loggins that. The only time it's about Iceman is when Slider's already got plans. How do you think that makes Iceman feel?

Silence of the Lambs

Hannibal Lecter: A census taker once tried to test me. I ate his liver with some fava beans and a nice_____.

A) Chianti

B) Diet Dr. Pepper

C) tall, frosty mug of let's-forget-I-ever-dated-Martha-Stewart

Dirty Dancing

Baby: Me? I'm scared of everything. I'm scared of what I saw, I'm scared of what I did, of who I am, and most of all I'm scared of walking out of this room

and_____.

A) never feeling the rest of my whole life the way I feel when I'm with you

B) getting a nose job that ruins my career

C) getting a nose job that ruins my love life

D) getting a nose job that ruins my looks

E) realizing I should have spent the money on my tits

Wall Street

Bud Fox: Blue Horseshoe loves_____.

A) Anacott Hookers

B) Anacott Cocaine

C) tiger blood

D) Anacott Steel

E) drinking water through his eyeball

F) shooting Kelly Preston in the arm

Star Wars Episode III, Revenge of the Sith

Anakin Skywalker: Are you all right? You're trembling. What's going on?

Padmé: Something wonderful has happened, Ani.

I'm_____.

A) pregnant

B) a ballerina

C) nominated for an Oscar

D) graduating from Harvard

E) a vegan

F) christening a baby gorilla at a Rwandan naming ceremony

G) rapping with Andy Samberg

H) still hot bald

I) on the cover of *Vogue*

J) campaigning for Obama

K) friends with Moby

L) winning an Olympic gold medal

M) discovering the goddamned cure for cancer

N) a dirty dirty dirty dirty dirty dirty whore

CASHMERE IS WASTED ON EVERYTHING BUT CELEBRITY THONGS

I just got a J.Crew catalog
In which
They are selling
A neon pink boys' cashmere sweater
So
If you're planning on buying this
Please let me know

I would love to come over to your house
And personally set your $178 on fire

DON'T STOP ON MY ACCOUNT

I was just strolling the baby
Around the block
When I came upon two men
Standing in an open garage
Yelling

"You're just like Dad. Full of anger and bitterness!"
"Oh, yeah?
Well at least I don't live with my head completely UP MY ASS!!"

On one hand, I was so sad
I thought about my sons
And wiped away a tear

Life is too short for resentment

But on the other hand
I thought:
Please
Go on
This is getting gooooood
You're on a roll
Bring up some shit about your mother, too

And holy crap

Did I go out "exercising" once again

Without a pen and paper?

NAILED IT

Mom

Come in here

You gotta see this TV show

Called Crocodile Hunter

It's about a UPS man

Who swims with iguanas

WHAT YOUR CELEBRITY CRUSH SAYS ABOUT YOU

Way back in 1987, before advanced sarcasm and leave-in conditioner were invented, I fell hard for my first celebrity crush: Jon Bon Jovi. Thanks to a publication called *Tiger Beat* -- which is nothing more than *Penthouse* for girls in headgear -- I knew Jon's full name (John Francis Bongiovi, Jr.), hometown (Sayreville, New Jersey), and hair length (14 inches). I also amassed several hundred tear-out posters of him that I lovingly plastered all over my school locker, bedroom walls, and regional highway overpasses. These were tearjerking pictures of Jon Bon posing in neon pantyhose, crossing his arms, and ferociously pouting because he obviously had yet to find the perfect, mildly-pubescent, Strawberry Shortcake connoisseur of his dreams.

This crush endured several decades -- despite his marriage, my marriage, and six children between us -- until I saw him interviewed in 2009 and witnessed him wearing what appeared to be PLEATED JEANS. Call me superficial, but within seconds, years of painful pining ended, I incinerated a Smithsonian's worth of *Tiger Beats*, and abruptly moved on to some dude who plays a synthesizer with one finger for some band I saw on *Saturday Night Live*.

Anyway, long story long, everyone has a celebrity crush (or 20) and most significant others will grant you the opportunity to sleep with this crush (or all 20) should the opportunity ever arise. The reason for this is not generosity. (Why, yes! Please have yourself a 72-hour lovefest with Ryan Reynolds! Don't let me stop you! How about I provide the Gatorade?) It's because it's NEVER GOING TO HAPPEN. There's a higher probability of Martha Stewart coming out with a line of edible thongs, than there is my husband getting propositioned by Angelina. So, by all means, Honey. Go for it.

Yes, given the improbability of Hollywood/civilian couplings, jealously only rears its head in certain cases. For me, it's when the celebrity being admired by my spouse is a celebrity I personally worship. Case in point: Kristen Wiig. When my husband fondly comments on one of her spastic dance moves, rest assured I do my best to compete by jitterbugging into a wall. (Isn't this hot, Dear? Isn't it? Huh? Huh? Crash. Bang. Whimpering.) On the flipside, I don't know which legend my husband aspires to be most like, but I'm going to pretend it's Abraham Lincoln. That way, I can send him out to buy a top hat while I watch a few Hugh Jackman movies.

Anyway, with all this said, what does your (or your significant other's) Hollywood infatuation reveal about you (or him/her)? I'm glad you asked. I happen to know A LOT about both psychology and famous people. As well as you and your mate. So, here you go:

Scarlett Johansson: You play the Powerball weekly, have Mount Everest on your bucket list, and know a lot about Chilean wine. Your Facebook cover photo is one of you ziplining in Costa Rica while wearing sunglasses that cost more than open heart surgery.

Ryan Gosling: You like to knit. And sob. You often stand in front of a full-length mirror with a handmade scarf and practice saying: "Here's a little something I made for you. Go on. Try it on. If you don't like it, I also made some grapefruit exfoliating scrub." You'd be better off going back to nursing school. Or bed.

Zooey Deschanel: You have a very low sperm count, but your spinach-artichoke dip is TO DIE FOR. In fact, rearrange those corn chips and let's snap some Instagram photos!

Prince Harry: You like camping, skeet, and blacking out. If you were a Disney princess, you'd be that one who takes her panties off on the Dumbo ride.

Natalie Portman: You have trouble differentiating between spoiled brats and murderers. You have no respect for *Star Wars*.

Spencer Pratt: Here's a bridge. Don't make me push you.

Jessica Simpson: You're a garden-variety jock who's saving up to hire someone to balance your checkbook. You're a boob guy and a butt guy. And also deaf.

Drew Barrymore: You like picnics, PETA, dotting your "i"s with daisies, and recreational coke.

Brad Pitt: Why, you must be the pillar of originality in your community. Let me guess: you enjoy walks on the beach and talking about the weather. Can I get you a salad with ranch on the side? Is your favorite music FM radio? Do you like to wear shirts? I thought so.

Beyonce: You're a completely delusional bookkeeper who still steals his father's Old Spice. Your favorite appetizer is mini corn dogs. You wear white socks with tassel loafers. You think Jay-Z is short for JCPenney.

Daniel Radcliffe: I'm calling the cops.

Gwyneth Paltrow: You're an awkward, nervous, well-meaning British man who answers to C-3PO.

Gael Garcia Bernal: What? You're not sure who this is? Good. All the better for me to try to explain it to you in broken Spanish so Gael can reach out, mash his pointer finger against my lips, and say: "Shhhhhhhhhh, my angel. Do not speak." Then while you're on **IMDB** looking up this fellow's filmography, he and I are eloping.

Eva Mendes: Congrats. You're alive.

(Originally appeared in a similar form on HowAboutWe)

PUMPING GAS

Please remove card quickly

Quickly?

Like how quickly?

This quickly?

Or quicker than that?

How long can I leave the card in there?

Oh

Never mind

I'm pretty sure my car just got pregnant

SO, NOT TODD AKIN?

Some non-controversial conversation topics for family, in-laws, and guests this holiday season: Steve Carrell, ginger ale, REO Speedwagon

Topics to avoid: mayonnaise brands, Ron Paul, the best way to get from here to there, corn syrup, Nancy Grace, the worst way to get from here to there, breast implants, hushpuppies, *The Help*, the *Old Farmer's Almanac*, sex, taxes, the Pope, razor blades, drawstring trash bags, thermostats, are cold sores herpes?, the price of gold, illiteracy, the care and maintenance of African violets, circumcision, almond milk, rape, where your grandmother's good china is.

NEVER MIND THE TSUNAMI OF BLOOD, WE'LL CUT YOU THE BEST DEAL ON SHAKER DINETTES

I get freaked out

By local kids

In local TV commercials

Trying to sell me stuff

It's like

The Shining twins

Trying to convince me their daddy

Has the best deal on mattresses

MOMMY'S TEN RULES OF MATH

1. Never, ever trouble yourself with any sort of math that involves the alphabet. Particularly because I have never seen a calculator with the ABCs anywhere on it. Except for "C." "C" means "erase" or "clear" and sometimes "off" and other times "on." See what I mean? Horribly bewildering. No. I don't know what "MC" means. I think it might be a leftover button from a fast food cash register.

2. "Percent" is American for the French "per cent," which means "for a copper penny." You know, that brown coin that we throw around willy-nilly in parking lots and fountains? You only need to know percents when it comes to milk and tipping. Here's an easy trick: always buy heavy cream and always leave five bucks. This will keep you healthy and wealthy. Also. You don't need to worry about percentages when it comes to sales. Macy's is always having a sale.

3. Short division and long division, as well as fractions, can be handled by most iPhone apps. Subdivisions? I try to avoid them. All the people wear Bermuda shorts and try to sell you Tupperware. You're better off renting a room in a hostel if you can't afford a city apartment.

4. If a train leaves one station going one speed and another train leaves another station going a different speed, I sure hope they serve wine because you kids never appreciate the journey. It's always about the damn destination and even then, when we arrive, you're still complaining. Merlot, please. Keep it comin'.

5. Pi is 3.14. What is Pi? I just told you. 3.14. Oh. You mean, what does 3.14 represent? Hmm. I think three of something with just a smidgen more of it. Like if you told someone you were going to see them in three weeks, but it was really more like 24 days instead of 21, you might say: "See you in Pi!"

6. Rulers, old-fashioned wooden ones, when rubbed furiously on the edge of your school desk, can start a small fire. If you're ever stranded on a desert island, be sure to take a desk and a ruler.

7. Movie math: MMMCCCCLXXXXV.

8. Pythagoras did NOT invent the Pythagoream Theorem. But he did believe people were reincarnated as vegetables. Like eggplants. What an idiot.

9. Don't worry, kids. When it comes to practical math, you really only need to know one thing: how to balance a checkbook. What's a checkbook, you ask? Well. It's made out of paper and flimsy plastic and is about the length of a King Size Hershey Bar

and it used to go in my purse, but has since been replaced by a debit card. What's a debit card? It's like a credit card, but it doesn't get you very far. Sometimes it has a little Snoopy hologram on it to make you feel better about being broke. Remember: you should always use your debit card to buy burritos and your credit card to buy vacations.

10. Lastly, don't get me wrong. Math anxiety is a very real, but very ridiculous illness. It is usualy cancelled out by a history slideshow or Spanish quiz and completely alleviated by the cafeteria's Taco Day. Oh, I forgot. You don't go to a school that has a cafeteria.

THE DARK SIDE

Son

You might appreciate knowing

That this Jedi apprentice braid

That I have painstakingly fashioned for you

Out of golden yarn per your insistence

Was first made popular

NOT by Obi Wan

But by Billy Ray Cyrus

Better known to your generation

As Hannah Montana's dad

Oh

I'm sorry

Did you just throw up?

Did I just ruin Star Wars for you?

I LOVE SURPRISES

Hey

Mom

I got your birthday present

But don't worry

I won't tell you what kind of animal

The ornament is but it's knitted

And we bought it at that same store

Where we also got that thing for your phone

That you've been wanting

PERSONAL JESUS

In the winter of 1994, I found myself snowed-in and melancholy on an Upstate New York campus, battling a stubborn angst that was based on a variety of things, including, but not limited to: a vitamin D deficiency, too much cheddar cheese, flabby thighs, a pet turtle I'd left over Christmas break at a Utica pet shop and subsequently abandoned, and the onerous quest for a boyfriend who was both a PoliSci major and ponytailed.

The pinnacle of this bleak chapter occurred one Friday in the college mailroom, where I received a package from my biological father after decades of silence. It was a soggy, crushed shirt-box upon which a Post-it note with my address had been Scotch-taped, and, going on looks alone, it appeared that the mangled parcel had made its way from the panhandle of Florida to the arctic moonscape of almost-Syracuse via pelican. A pelican who had decided to swallow the Dillard's box somewhere over, say, Indiana and then finally shit it out in an exhaust-covered snowdrift near the Student Center.

Inside, was a single piece of department store tissue paper and a crocheted, cropped sweater that was equal parts potholder and shawl. A perplexing piece of knitwear-meets-housewares that was in dire need of a camisole. Which unfortunately, along with any sort of note, had not been included.

All of this really belongs in another essay titled "Deadbeat Dads Do The Darnedest Things," but I mention it because it was the tipping point for me that winter. And in what felt like a major act of rebellion against the backdrop of my communal dorm -- where I lived and cooked with 50 vegetarians independent of the college's room-and-board plan (a place where boys were known to wear skirts and girls were known to wear armpit hair) -- I shut myself into the first-floor phone booth, called the deep south, and requested a counselor application for a religious summer camp.

I was raised as a moderate, border state Episcopalian, but after six years on decidedly agnostic turf in mostly Connecticut and New York, there was little evidence of this left, save for a hidden monogrammed sweater and an innate guilt that kept me more or less in the realm of third base -- a sexual shortstop, so to speak.

That said, I was poorly equipped to lead a cabin full of adolescent girls in a nightly Bible-based prayer circle. Nor was I in any way qualified to teach archery for eight weeks. But that's what I was assigned in June: a hut full of deadly weapons and a cabin of nine 13-year-olds in various stages of puberty who had all kinds of questions about both Jesus and their vaginas.

I think the first night's devotion went something like this:

Me: Hi! Welcome to camp! Tonight's topic is The Golden Rule.

Camper 1: Was Jesus real?

Me: Ummmmm.....................Yes?

Camper 2: How do you know?

Me: Well. Because archaeologists have, you know, found stuff?

Camper 3: Like what kind of stuff?

Me: Uhhhh.......Papyrus?

Camper 4: Do you smoke? Because I found a lighter in your toiletry bag.

Camper 5: I think she smokes.

Camper 6: My mommy rubs my back before bed.

Camper 7: Have you ever tried stuffing your bra?

Archery wasn't much better. My assistant wore a side ponytail with a sorority logo-emblazoned ribbon that matched her sorority logo-emblazoned shirt that matched her sorority logo-emblazoned sandals and clipboard and ballpoint pen. She was nice in a forced sort of way (that suggested she always ended up ugly-crying when drunk), and easily -- oh-so-easily -- disgusted. Ooh gnats! Ooh chiggers! Ooh I just found out that there's something called a scrotum!

I didn't tell her I'd founded my own eight-person sorority up north, which had also initiated one housecat and a gay guy and was named Alpha Alpha Hydroxy after a wrinkle cream. But I did break her in on day three with the old plastic-dogshit-in-the-quiver joke. How she and I had ended up together and in charge of lethal equipment, I'll never know. But if it was God's will, he's probably working on the Martha Stewart/Russell Brand ammunition kiosk as we speak.

I'm not sure what Jesus thought of all this. That is, I'm not sure what certain Jesuses thought of all this. Because I quickly saw that there were several, different, smaller Jesus camps within the larger Jesus camp as a whole. Here are a some of the Jesuses I observed and silently named:

The Great Scoutmaster
Teva Jesus
Farmer J
God Jr.
Coach Christ
Republican Charles Ingalls Jesus
and Bearded Fabio

These were the Jesi of choice by the following groups, respectively: competitive badge earners, Dave Matthews groupies, rednecks, Baptists, softball players and/or closet lesbians, Delta Delta Deltas, and the two British gals who ran the tack room.

Having a personal Jesus was a fascinating idea. The notion of fine-tuning my Higher Power -- from an oversized Wilford Brimley who'd had it up to HERE with my aviation phobia, into someone I could actually relate to -- resonated in way I'm guessing Build-A-Bear does for tweens.

With that in mind, I began to imagine a God who was okay with poor posture, practical jokes involving dogshit (definitely plastic, possibly real), and occasional-but-not-repetitive playing of Cypress Hill. A God who would cut me some slack on certain lesser sins, such as beer bongs, compulsive swearing, and my hatred for Helen Hunt. Slowly, my Jesus began to take shape, only to end up looking not unlike George Carlin.

So, I made some modifications, adding the heart of a Kindergarten teacher and the hair of Jennifer Aniston, until my imaginary Jesus looked too much like *Full House*'s Lori Loughlin and required a hearty dose of Robert Plant's passion and Jerry Seinfeld's wit. Still not completely satisfied, I added a dash of Val Kilmer and a sprinkle of Chevy Chase and that unexplainable sex appeal of Steve Martin until the Jesus in my head looked so fucked up that I just quit.

But anyway, to bring this thing full-circle, the best thing I took away from that summer -- other than a personal Jesus who I have finally realized is actually pretty much John Cusack with two sheep under his arms and the eyes of Colin Farrell and the soul of Mother Teresa (that ponytailed PoliSci guy after all) -- is that some kids get really shitty care packages.

I mean, most kids that summer got comic books and *Seventeen* and hidden chocolates and eye shadows sets. But a chosen few got smashed envelopes of used sponge rollers. Or half-empty bottles of Avon sunscreen. Or eucalyptus cough drops.

One girl's father even sent her some prunes in a Ziploc. And let me tell you: prunes in a Ziploc don't look so good after shipment.

I told that camper, "Hey. I feel your pain. I got a really crappy package once, too."

"Really?"

"Yes. It was placemat. Or maybe a tank top. Or maybe a cat hammock. I don't really know." The camper looked down at her prunes, and I felt like this was where I was supposed to bring religion into the picture. "Listen," I said. "It could be worse. I mean, instead of prunes, your dad could have sent you something else. Such as to die," I lowered my voice, "FOR ALL OF HUMANITY'S SINS."

The girl thought about that long and hard. I watched her face as she considered her dried fruit. I felt like something big was clicking. Because, I mean, in that moment, something seemed to for me. Such as, if certain people and certain papyruses were to be believed, there was someone who looked a lot like George Carlin's sister who loved me more than my own mother did. Which meant that every time I thought about that piece of knit-shit doily titsling that the pelican had expelled, I could give thanks I'd gotten a wearable oven mitt and not crucified. Which was sort of huge. If you can bring yourself to believe.

I looked again at the camper.

"These aren't prunes," she said. "They're dates."

"What?!"

"These are dates."

"So, that's what you've taken away from all this?" I asked.

To which, she shrugged and I slumped on the cabin floor.

Jesus Christ.

(Originally appeared in a similar form on Loop)

THIS BAKED POTATO COULD KILL SOMEONE

Hey. Microwave.

What's up with you and your shitty-ass math skills?

Because when I press in 100

You think that means 60 seconds

And when I press in 300

You think that means three minutes, which is actually 180 seconds, and not 300 seconds

Do you think you can just rewrite the way all of humanity counts?

Do you think you can decide that if my Bagel Bites want to be nuked 500 seconds that you can turn that into five minutes, which is actually 300 seconds and thus take 200 damn seconds off the processing of my miniature pizza?

You are so bold and so stupid.

You're like the Dina Lohan of appliances.

INTERNET SHOPPING

Would I like to VIEW ALL?

No thanks

I'd rather only see four or five gifts

Of someone's entire online gift registry

That way

When I am on page 98

I'll have no idea what page that coffee maker was on

So

Thanks for asking, Macy's

But VIEW ALL

Is for lazy shits

GO PLAY ON THE WHORE

I never tire of telling kids
To go jump on the tramp

(She's was quite a deal
We got her at Sam's Club for $300
And she lives under the mimosa tree)

THE NATIONAL ANNOYANCE LEVEL CHART

Sometimes, it can be difficult to differentiate between that which is mildly annoying and moderately annoying, and between that which is moderately annoying and severely annoying. But the threat of pending annoyance and/or imminent annoyance is always present. The National Annoyance Level Chart has been devised expressly for our citizens -- to clarify and simplify the many levels of annoyance -- so they will know, with utmost certainty, the difference between mildly and moderately annoying, and between moderately and severely annoying, as well as what qualifies as: faintly annoying, kinda annoying, really annoying, egregiously annoying, and downright up-the-ass annoying.

Faintly Annoying
Plaid tams, Grandparents' Day, Art Garfunkle, hiccups, baby corn, lint, ambrosia salad

Mildly Annoying
bongos, Flipper, Reduced Sodium Triscuits, Rick Dees, buckteeth, Belgium

Kinda Annoying
Groupon, dingleberries, Ke$ha, The Hamburglar, Roomba, windchimes

Moderately Annoying

gnats, Jim Cantore, polka dots, Puerto Rico, pinworms

Really Annoying

tenor saxophones, poppyseeds, *A Chorus Line*, rosacea, Ziggy, knee replacement, cats' assholes

Severely Annoying

PT Cruisers, blue balls, Shirley Temple, possums, Blues Traveler, glaucoma

Egregiously Annoying

scabies, Kelly Ripa, CAPS LOCK, mustard gas, French vanilla candles, vuvuzelas, the elderly

Downright Up-The-Ass Annoying

Rachael Ray, brain tumors

I JUST DON'T GET IT

The electrician
Who is working on our doorbell
Just said he needed to go to
Radio Shack for a part

Once again
Reminding me
That somehow Radio Shack
Has cornered the market
On shit Lowe's hasn't figured out how to sell

HOW ABOUT WHEN I'M IRONING?

I find it disturbing when someone dies a tragic and untimely
death
And someone says:
At least he died doing what he loved

WHAT?!?!?!?!

I do NOT want to DIE doing something I LOVE
Here's when to kill me:
When I am writing a thank-you note
for a brown, shag BATHMAT
That's a good time to come up behind me
with some piano wire
And sever my windpipe

But if I'm ever doing something I love
Such as wearing a beer hat
filled with champagne
while I'm giving Johnny Depp a leisurely sponge bath
That is NOT an optimum time for a blood vessel to explode in
my brain

If that's how I go
People better march in the goddamned streets for two weeks in

my honor

Lower that flag to half staff

People better be saying:

Did you hear?!

How she went?!

THE HORROR

(Collective sobs. Faces in palms. Dry heaves.)

If that's how I die,

People better declare it a national holiday.

The kind of somber holiday people won't even take off work for

They'll just sit at their desks

And stare out the window

And wonder how this world could be so cruel

I CAN SAY THE WORD "KARATE"
IN FOUR LANGUAGES

One time
In Paris
I ordered a grilled cheese
And ended up having a gun held to my temple

No
Just kidding
They summoned a urologist

And once
In Italy
I ordered a chef's salad
And they brought me an octopus
Dead
But whole
In a pool of olive oil

I mean
I think it was olive oil

WAAAAAY-TOO-PERSONAL ADS

Poorly paid middle manager, 40, still scared of father, seeks wet nurse.

Heavily medicated SWF, who can no longer achieve orgasm unless whipped with a garden hose by a man wearing a Regis Philbin mask, seeks investment banker-type to tell me my feet aren't ugly. My favorite maxi pad is Kotex.

Divorced male, 34, seeks companion, 25-40. Likes: racial jokes, Topsiders, turning over the dining room table when your run-of-the-mill meatloaf is placed before me. Dislikes: Grandmothers, bathing.

DBF seeks athletic male, 30-65. I like triathlons, antiques, and discussing bowel movements. Very adventurous. Why, just last week, I ate my niece's placenta.

Widowed male, 84. Extremely depressed. I have white pubic hair and very little money.

Trust fund prick, 32, seeks SWF with my stepsister's ass.

Bipolar receptionist with 60K credit card debt, 80K student loan debt, 4 beagles, and anemia seeks wealthy man with pancreatic cancer who doesn't mind sleeping on the couch while I sleep upstairs wrapped in my Sebastian Bach poster.

SJF, 29, seeks educated SJM. I suck my thumb but nothing else. In certain lighting, I also have a beard.

Fundamentalist Christian male seeks Paul Ruebens lookalike who does a spot-on Carol Channing impersonation.

Former stripper seeks creative type to feed me baby food.

Psoriasis-riddled SWM seeks fun! I have a thing for amputees and suffer from IBS. In high school, I intentionally killed a parrot with household explosives. I deal pot. I cry in my sleep. I never leave home without my Preparation H in a front-facing fanny pack. I'm looking for a lady under 90 pounds to check my back for suspicious moles. Do you love swing dancing followed by three-minute sex? Let's make magic.

FROM THE BACKSEAT

How much does a tire weigh?

Why don't they make cheese soda?

Do birds scream when their feathers fall out?

How many days till I die?

Just think. That windshield is covered in germs.

Tsunamis never hit Nebraska.

Hey! What's a scab made of?

If you hold in your poop long enough, it just gets stored in your leg.

WHAT'S FOR DINNER?

Tonight

I've prepared

Everyone

Individually-sized

Shut your chicken pot pieholes

IS ENYA ONE PERSON OR TWO? (LIKE I CARE.)

The whole time

I was getting that facial

They were playing the Fresh Market soundtrack

All I kept thinking was

Put down the $12 cheese

Put down the $12 cheese

Put down the $12 cheese

REALLY. YOU SHOULDN'T HAVE.

There are lots of bars in my personal history that I fondly, if
somewhat hazily, recall: Don's Rok of my college years -- a
Clinton, New York dive where I drank dollar Saranacs like baby
formula, played habitual billiards, and perfected party tricks such
as putting my entire fist in my mouth and falling off tables to
Bachman-Turner Overdrive. If memory serves, James Brown's
"Sex Machine" was 3902 on the jukebox, and, when I
graduated, I wrote the bartenders a thank-you note on engraved
stationery. Because that's what borderline rehab-eligible girls with
good Southern manners do...

...WRITE BARTENDERS THANK-YOU NOTES.

Then, in Florida, there's Roscoe's, where we go for good laughs
while on vacation. In that tiki tavern, you can always find
musician Kent Taylor Brown wailing on an electric piccolo while
widows in dentures play grab-ass. My husband and I enjoy sitting
in the corner with a couple of Coors Lights and watching old
folks pop Viagra and throw out their backs to "Aqualung." It's
reassuring to know that people who have to put their steak in a
blender are still getting laid.

And then there's The Clover Club.

The Clover Club is a West Virginia establishment that clings to the mountainside like a dingleberry to an ass. Inside, a rambling bar made up of cheap folding tables, folding chairs, a dance floor, and catwalk provides plenty of room for several hundred Appalachians to get their freak on -- which they regularly do at one of the many theme nights advertised on the roadside marquee. Themes like: Foam Party, Homemade Bikini Contest, and Midget Wrestling. This is a place genius enough to put shag carpeting in the bathroom. Deep shag. So, as you can imagine, The Clover Club smells like a sperm bank where Ace Frehley's wig has been used for a barf bag.

Nearby, my parents have a vacation home at a prestigious resort. But when I take my posse of girls over to West Virginia, we aren't so good at wearing madras and playing croquet. No, the last time we were there we drove through the golf course blasting "Drop It Like It's Hot," took a skeet lesson (drunk), and then, to save a little money, we cancelled our dinner reservation and headed to the Clover Club Ladies' Night on empty stomachs.

It didn't occur to us that Ladies' Night might attract fewer ladies who wanted to watch men take their clothes off and more ladies who wanted to watch other ladies who wanted to watch men take their clothes off. In short, there were us eight girls, maybe another 12 like us, and, oh, 150 or so West Virginian lesbians. Hulking, powerful, professional lesbians who drove trucks and strangled white-tailed deer for a living. These ladies were crammed around the many folding tables, leaning on Paul Bunyan arms and sporting Niagara Falls-size mullets. They smoked Duraflame logs in lieu of cigarettes. They drank beers out of construction barrels. They wore army tents for mini skirts. I think one of them even had an anaconda in her hair instead of a scrunchie. Long story medium length, these badass bitches were there to find someone like me (a girl about the size of Webster) who they could buy a half dozen lemon drops before subsequently using as a tampon.

Anyway, the night's entertainment was supposed to involve a group of young, male strippers from Manhattan -- a group that, from their poster, looked just like the Chippendales, minus the bow ties but plus the HPV. However, after about an hour, the only stripper who'd made it in for the act was a guy named Dante. Dante was tall, lanky, completely hairless, and looked like he might have just finished the seventh grade. He was charming and nervous in his t-shirt and jeans, and someone needed to just go on and arrest all of us in the bar for expecting him to take off his underwear instead of finishing his book report. His boss, some 50-something Italian dude named Lenny, came out on the catwalk to introduce Dante and to inform us that, since the rest of the seventh grade boys hadn't gotten their permission slips signed, he'd be filling in. Which is kind of like having a garbageman jump out of a cake.

I don't remember what Dante did. Probably normal stripper shit like dancing around in a thong and throwing his chaps at the crowd. Why don't I remember? Well, for one, Lenny set right to work putting on a show that involved a cookie sheet and lighter fluid. He just walked out on the runway, fat and shirtless in a pair of leather pants, threw a fucking broiler pan on the floor, sprayed it with butane, tossed a match on that bitch, ripped off his velcro pants to reveal a metal-studded g-string, and then crouched over the flaming cookie sheet and swayed his balls around for a few minutes. To coax the flame into a real blaze, he got out an old, white washcloth, and swirled it around, too.

I mean, at that point, I think I just started waving at Pauline Bunyan, and screaming, "Here's your tampon!"

The second reason I don't remember what Dante did is because right after Lenny's tribute to Betty Crocker, he yanked me out of my chair and onto the stage, bent me over, put an inflated balloon against the seat of my jeans, and just started pretend power-sodomizing me. Halfway through this uproarious crowd-pleaser, he explained this was a fun gag they did with the ladies until the balloon popped. Well, goddamned NASA must have made that balloon, because I think it took close to 18 minutes for the fucker to give. The good news is, the audience seemed to really enjoy watching Lou Ferrigno have faux anal with the mom from *Family Ties*.

After that, I started trying to herd the eight of us to the parking lot. I'd only gotten one Bud Light in me, what with all the comedic buttsex, and I was burning rubber out of there. One of my friends, drunker than I have ever seen anyone, just looked at me stone-cold homicidal and said, in what I think was the slowest of slow-motion: "FUUUUUUUUUUUUCCCCCCKKKKKK YOOOOUUUUUUUUUUU." So, she stayed. Another suggested that we take advantage of the "complimentary Clover Club limo." Which I'd seen on the way in and was nothing more than a piece of stretch herpes. A third friend was busy paying Dante $10 to dance with her. And a fourth was maybe looking in the shag for her dignity. The remaining four of us made it out to the parking lot where my car alarm was blaring.

"I wonder how long that's been going off," someone asked.

"Ever since Lenny put a dent in this here asscheek!!!" I screamed, removing my car keys from my back pocket.

Back at the house, somebody choked on an ice cube. Somebody put three cold pizzas in the oven but didn't turn it on. And another girl did a face plant into the open freezer where she landed on a bag of frozen peas. I think she stayed there till morning. The other four made it home very late, in various stages of toxicity. As for me, I closed out the evening by finally getting serious about some beer and writing Lenny a thank-you note.

(Originally appeared in a similar form on Loop)

THIS WEEK ON THE REAL HOUSECATS OF AKRON

Tabitha starts drinking toilet water.

Chablis sleeps with Hellweasel.

Jinglebell and Falafel go on a catnip bender.

Doughdaddy poops in a ficus plant.

Poptart, aka Miss Stinkers, has lunch with Nicole Itchy and
Purris Hilton.

Velvet releases a Christian pop single.

Butterscotch starts sexting Kelsey Grammer.

Bethenny Frankel gets declawed.

I'LL TAKE IT

Yesterday

I was pushing a huge pot of baked beans

In the stroller

To a street party

When an old man

With a patch over one eye

Whistled at me

DO YOU KNOW YOUR AMANDA RIGHTS?

You have the right to remain silent. You have the right to whisper. You have the right to talk all damn day just so long as I don't have to care. Or pretend I care.

You have the right to borrow my green cardi. And my thermal henley. But not my J.Crew hoodie. You know how much a J.Crew hoodie will set you back? Do you? That's right. I didn't think so.

You have the right to say something "stinks." But not that something "sucks." Because when you say something "sucks" it will make people think you're a common whore. Unless you actually are one. And if that's the case, then just go on and say something "blows."

You DO NOT have the right to say the word "retarded." Because it's totally mean. I mean you can use it when you're referring to math homework and school chicken patties and Crocs and knock-off Prada and your locker combination and the game of softball and country music and your retainer But don't use it when you're referring to people, except for those retards Tania Barrington and Wendy Schultz and Carlie Peebles.

You also can't say something is "so gay." Except for *That's So Raven* and chem class and Nelson Masterson. They ARE "so gay." No doubt.

You have the right to eat bananas in the lunchroom if they're cut up and dipped in fat-free peanut butter and eaten with a fork. But at all costs avoid corndogs and Popsicles. Unless, once again, you're a common whore. Which I'm beginning to think you are.

You have the right to look at me and I have the right to look straight through you. Has anyone seen my lip gloss?

You have the right to look at my breasts. Aren't they pretty?

You do NOT have the right to look at my butt. Were you looking at my butt? Sick. What's wrong with you?

You have the right to copy answers off my history test and fail miserably.

You have a right to ask me to prom and I have the right to think about it for as long as it takes that other guy to get up the nerve to ask me.

You have the right to come to my slumber party, but only if you bring gin in a shampoo bottle. Don't tell anyone I invited you.

We'll just pretend you showed up and I'll pretend to feel sorry for you. Then you'll hand me the gin and I'll drink it all myself. Don't bother bringing a sleeping bag.

You have the right to come visit me while I'm working at the Hawaiian Ice shack. But I can't give you a free sample. Unless, of course, you brought more gin.

You have the right to call me Amanda. You have the right to call me Mandy. But you don't have the right to call me. Or email me. Or wave to me from across the library. Or slip me a note during study hall. Texts only, please.

(Originally appeared in a similar form on The Big Jewel)

NEW YEAR'S RESOLUTIONS
FOR THE EXTREMELY MOTIVATED

Change all your Internet passwords to include both letters and numbers and at least two symbols, such as % or $ or #, and be sure to use at least 12 characters

Stop screaming at yourself in the mirror

Take down half the tree

BRUCE WILLIS SEEMS HAPPY

I think everything went to hell for Demi Moore

When she quit singing for Journey

On that note,

I wonder if Steve Perry

Watches old episodes of Moonlighting

When he's depressed

UNCOMPROMISING POSITIONS

I tend to believe that besides humility, humor, and bags of diamonds, what a couple shares in common is what keeps them together. Keep in mind that my opinion is not scientifically based -- I got my degree in Reverse Psychology -- but when my husband and I do things we both enjoy, we're much happier -- both as individuals and as a pair.

It took us a while to figure this out, because a lot of well-meaning people (who have obviously endured years of torture and want you to do the same) will tell you that you should do what the other partner enjoys doing, even if you DESPISE it, because if you're a good mate that sort of sacrifice will bring you great joy.

Please.

If I somehow agree to attend (read: get drugged, hogtied, and pushed in a wheelbarrow to) a football game, euphoric confetti could shoot from my husband's eyes, and I will still feel like someone is disemboweling me with an ice cream scoop. If you ask me, if there is a hell, it probably looks a lot like the Alamodome.

On the flipside, if you ever see my husband accompanying me to buy and discuss cropped jeans, rest assured he has sold our children for a hologram of himself.

Years ago, we finally realized the futility of the "I'll do something you like, then you do something I like" theory when we were sightseeing in Boston and had some sort of seething feud over the Freedom Trail and the New England Aquarium. I don't remember the details, but I think it involved beluga whales and strangling. Making up involved a patriotic amount of Sam Adams, and at some point in our intoxication we remembered that we both liked biking. So after we recovered from a hangover of colonial proportions, we spent the remainder of the trip cycling from Cape Cod to Nantucket and -- shocker -- GETTING ALONG.

For me, it was a great relief to quit pretending I enjoyed the driving range, Christopher Nolan movies, and lamb stew. And my husband has never been so glad to give up Tarot readings, Scattergories, and almond milk (though, honestly? That jackass has no idea what he's missing). And now, when together, we focus primarily on joint likes, such as: *Deadliest Catch*, hiding from our children, grilling animals, Louis CK, the musical stylings of the Ray Conniff Singers, and inventing dishes for Paula Deen. Why, we could spend the better part of an evening one-upping one another with phrases like "may-uh-naise margaritas" and "medallions of booder in clarified booder." (Obviously, we should write a book on romance.)

Anyway, my point is: couples should do lots of things together that they both like and very few things together that only one likes. (It should also be noted that if the things you agree on most are methamphetamines or not touching each other, you might need professional help.)

And also: let's not forget that if you both DON'T LIKE something, it can be as wonderful as both LIKING something. During basketball season, my husband will often reach across the dinner table and take my hand, only to whisper: "We'll always have our hatred for Duke." Be still my beating heart. He always knows the right thing to say.

(Originally appeared in a similar form on HowAboutWe)

SOMEBODY FOUND A CONDOM
IN THE TUBE SLIDE

A picnic at the park
Is not a picnic at the park
Until somebody steps on a discarded chicken cutlet
And gets it completely embedded
In their sneaker treads

Or until you see a father in pajama bottoms
Wearing a "Dirty Dick's Crab Shack" t-shirt
And carrying a floral diaper bag

Or until you see three teens
From afar
Wearing black wigs
Doing something with a bucket
And filming themselves with a videocamera

It's probably a school-related project
But from here
It looks like the overdose of Liza Minnelli
And the subsequent mourning of her
Overweight twin sisters

MOMMY? WHY DON'T YOU EVER GET EMBARRASSED?

(Hmmmm.

Do I tell my child about last week's open mic

Where my vas deferens joke was met with utter silence?

Or do I bring up the time I was asked to be a model

For a flat-chested women's website?

Or do I mention ripping my stirrup pants

While singing Brass Monkey?

Or do I discuss vaginal birth?)

Son

The answer is

Mommy doesn't get embarrassed

Because years of humiliation

Have brought about a liberating sense of apathy.

Now

When I get out of the car

Will you tell me if I have sat in chocolate again?

SOMETIMES SHE EVEN BUYS A PRETZEL

Today will mark my third consecutive day
To not only the mall
But the Crocs kiosk

I think
This might qualify me for some part on a
Bravo reality show

It would be a show about a woman
Who can never buy her child the right size shoe

But most of the series would just show
Parking lot security camera footage
Of her giving a rusty umbrella stroller
The finger

IT'S LIKE...

I have a bone to pick with everyone who had children before me. A bone roughly the size of a Tyrannosaurus Rex's femur. When I was childless and naïve, none of the veteran parents I came in contact with had the decency to offer up a few analogies for the trials of parenthood. Not one measly simile did I receive.

Actually, I retract that statement. I think a stroller-pushing gal at the video store compared morning sickness to seasickness -- which is kind of like saying being hit by a coal truck is akin to being grazed by a wayward shuttlecock. But the rest of the moms and dads out there? Well, they just smiled and said things like: a baby will make you tired.

"How tired?" I remember asking.

"Tired."

"Just tired?"

"No. Tired tired."

It didn't sound like a very terrible tired at the time -- just like an exaggerated drowsy. Possibly the way one might feel after sipping sherry in a hammock. Or having a conversation with a mannequin. Or watching a documentary on the unabridged history of the spatula.

But I soon learned otherwise. The tired in question was the great-grandfather of exhaustion. What those parents should have said was:

"Oh, you'll be tired. Honolulu-to-Hong Kong-by-way-of-London jetlag tired. On top of downing-a-handful-of-Ambien-and-scaling-Mount Everest-in-flip-flops tired. You'll be so tired you'll call 9-1-1 and ask for a Meat Lover's, then call Pizza Hut and ask for a stretcher. You'll be so cross-eyed fried that if you happen to go to a funeral in your sleep-deprived state, you'll be thrown out. For crawling into the casket and spooning with the dearly departed."

No one put it to me that way. And really, they should have. Because now, with a 3-year-old who's had jaundice, colic, acid reflux, ear tubes, 30 colds, 12 ear infections, several choking incidents, 14 rounds of crying-it-out, seven unidentified rashes, a mysterious skull lump that required X-rays and ultrasounds, not to mention a Hollywood-level addiction to Infant Motrin and fire engines (specifically the ever-elusive pumper/tanker), I can say from experience that the best and possibly only way to describe something as indescribable as parenthood is not to say what it is, but what it's like.

For example, I would have appreciated knowing that administering oral medication to an infant was about as easy as inserting a rectal suppository into a hummingbird. I would have also liked to have known that bathing a baby was like trying to wrestle a greased eggplant from Lake Superior. And in lieu of another sterling rattle, I would have much preferred the gift of blatant honesty. Why didn't someone tell me that diapering a baby boy was the equivalent of folding an origami crane while someone urinated in my mouth?

Perhaps it would have behooved my husband and me to have attended a Parenting Simulation Seminar. Lord knows, the "Baby Boot Camp" we did attend, put on by the hospital and complete with stale Pringles and birthing videos, did nothing more than make my husband blush and me cross my legs.

No, what we could have used was a morning spent shepherding a half dozen raccoons to the roller rink. And an afternoon with a flying squirrel at the opera. And an evening convincing a leprechaun he really wanted an enema in exchange for yo-yo.

Lastly, we could have capped it all off with the saddest of predicaments: being too tired to drink.

Had we had the pleasure of those activities, we might have known what birthday parties and church and the dentist and most every night for the foreseeable future were really going to be like.

But, please. If such a workshop existed, you think anyone would sign up?

Me neither.

Because without also simulating the sheer wonder and joy and love of parenthood, it would all seem pointless. Which brings me to a different realm of analogies -- the good ones. Every parent knows it might be challenging to describe labor (pooping a disco ball comes to mind). But it's harder to describe the wondrous things: the ultrasounds, your baby's first smile, the utter hilarity of conversations with a 3-year-old. And it's downright impossible, with or without the time-tested simile, to describe the adoration of a parent.

Before my son was born, I loved my dog. In a way that felt to me at the time like genuine parental love.

"You'll forget the dog when the baby's born," people said. "The love you feel for that dog has nothing on the love you'll feel for your child."

I scoffed. I didn't believe them. I believed that not only must my dog be far superior to their dogs, but my heart must be, too.

Then my son was born and they were right. The love I felt for him was in an entirely different league than the love I felt for Buddy. With his first gurgle, the baby moved Buddy's status on the affection meter down to that of a taco salad. A good taco salad. One with homemade guacamole. But a taco salad nonetheless.

It's easy to compare the hard stuff to other hard stuff. It's easy to say there's not much difference between putting a onesie on a squirming baby than a condom on a ferret. Feeding my son his first few bowls of rice cereal was indeed much like sitting in front of an oscillating fan into which someone dumped wallpaper paste. And please, it would be much quicker for me to give a howler monkey a bikini wax than to try and clip all 20 of the baby's fingernails and toenails while he's awake.

But the devotion I feel toward my son? It escapes comparison. And perhaps that is why all those veteran parents refrained from giving it to me straight. Knowing what I was headed for, both tortuous and divine, did they really want to be honest? How effective would it have been to say to me:

"You think they've got it bad at Guantanamo Bay? Just you wait. After averaging 45 minutes of sleep a day, gotten in 90-second intervals, you'll be begging for grade-D mutton and Christina Aguilera on continuous loop. Parenting can be hell."

"What?" I would have gasped. "Hell?"

"That's right."

"Then why do it?" I would have asked.

"Because," the seasoned parent would sigh, searching for a way to explain. "It's also heaven."

And it's true. If having to parent is hellish, then being a parent is heavenly.

Don't get me wrong. I still think all those parents-to-be deserve a little honesty. They deserve to know that colic can squash your sanity faster than a silverback gorilla can an overripe banana And that putting a feisty 1-year-old into a car seat is about as easy as getting a pound of cooked linguine back into the box. But also try your best to tell them what the love is like, even if searching for an analogy turns you into a stammering Valley Girl.

"It's like…it's like…it's like…Awesome."

EVERY NIGHT, IT'S THE SAME

Put the children to bed!

Get the children in their pajamas!

Pick out a story and some non-flouride toothpaste and some
underwear that doesn't itch and some crackers served sans cheese
on a formula lid and some water sipped from a bath toy for the
love of all things sacred!!!!!

GOOD GOD!!!!!

SOMEONE MAKE THESE CHILDREN CLOSE THEIR
GODFORSAKEN MOUTHS AND EYES!!!!!

Put on your PJ Harveys!

IT'S BEDTIME FOR BONZO!

Why won't this pajama shirt fit over your Big Head Todd and
The Monsters?

Do you see a monster?

NO!!!!!

Other than the woman who birthed you?

NO!!!!!

There are no monsters

Trust me

Other than this satanic beast called

MOM

Who is fumbling for the light switch

And then
When all has been hosed down
And I'm having a glass of wine
And looking out over the smoldering remains of bedtime
I think

There now
That wasn't so hard now

Was it?

IF THIS HAMSTER EVER DIES

I won't be able to tell

By smell alone

Thank you for buying, looking at, picking up, and/or possibly even reading this book. I really appreciate it. If you want to buy another one or know more about me or my writing, you can visit: www.whitneycollins.com